W9-DHS-404

DALLAS SPIRIT

A Political History of the City of Dallas

───────── ❖ ─────────

By Allison A. Cheney

Dallas Spirit

Copyright © 1991 by Allison A. Cheney

All rights reserved.

No part of this book may be reproduced without written permission of the author.

Library of Congress Cataloging in Publication Data

ISBN No. 0-9630215-0-8

First Printing 1991

Published by McMullan Publishing Co.
Dallas, Texas

Printed by Taylor Publishing Co.
Dallas, Texas

ACKNOWLEDGEMENTS

I'd like to recognize the following Texas politicians who confirmed my belief that most elected officials are honest and sincere and want to make the world a better place: Mayor Wes Wise, Mayor Annette Strauss, Mayor Jack Evans, Governor Ann Richards, Congressman Jim Collins, Representative Dick McKissack, Senator Lloyd Bentsen, Judge Ron Chapman, Congressman John Bryant, District Attorney Henry Wade, and State Comptroller John Sharp.

My sincere thanks:

To the following teachers who inspired me in journalism, history, and government: Dr. June Welch, Dr. Alexandra Wilhelmsen, Dr. Frank Swietek, Lydia Haggar Novakov, and Mary Lou Dix.

To my family for their support especially my mother, Nancy Goff Cheney, my aunt Dixie Cheney Prater, and my aunt Janey Goff McIntire, who spent many late nights editing this manuscript.

To Helen Lance, publishing consultant, and Mike McCauley, legal advisor, whose advice was invaluable.

To the staff at the J. Erik Jonsson Library, whose assistance in obtaining materials made this book possible.

To my colleagues at KZPS/KAAM radio, whose faith in me is so appreciated, especially: Tom Glade, Buz Powers, Danny Owen, Jaan McCoy, and Bill Koeninger.

And most importantly, I'd like to thank former Dallas Mayor Wes Wise, my friend and mentor, who is always there when I need him.

*I dedicate this book to the memory
of my grandfather*

Bobby Goff,

whose love and pride of Dallas inspired me.

FOREWORD

I have been active in Dallas politics all of my life. My first job in a campaign was stuffing envelopes when I was five years old. My family was always involved in one campaign or another. As I grew older, I became even more interested in politics. I've worked on local, state, and national elections for many years.

My love for Dallas began when I was a little girl sitting on my grandfather's lap hearing him tell about the early days of Dallas. He was born here in 1902, and it was through him that I first recognized what Dallas spirit was: a complete feeling of pride and an attitude of vigor and courage. He would drive me downtown and show me the Cumberland Hill School that he attended shortly after the turn of the century, Reverchon Park where he played sandlot baseball as a young boy, and across the viaduct to where Burnett Field once stood when he managed the Dallas Eagles during the heyday of the Texas League. He told me many fond stories about the people and places of Dallas when it was a small town and everyone knew everyone. Many people I speak of in this book were his close friends, especially the city leaders whom he assured me accepted their positions because they sincerely wanted to make Dallas the very best place to live in the country.

As a student at the University of Dallas, I wrote a thesis on the political history of the city of Dallas. My professor, Dr. June Welch, urged me to turn my thesis into a book since there is no such publication available. The problem was when and where do you stop writing history? I decided the 150th birthday of our city would be the best time to end this phase of Dallas history.

This book is primarily the history of Dallas politics and

the spirit and vision of our community leaders from John Neely Bryan to Annette Strauss. I have added some additional history of a few businesses, industries, institutions, and personalities showing the same spirit that all of the people of Dallas possess — to name them all would be impossible.

I don't believe there is a city in the world that commands the love and respect of its citizens like Dallas. Those of us whose families have been here for generations feel deeply that Dallas belongs to us, yet we are willing to share our beautiful city with newcomers and we know that they will find a city of compassion and love of fellow man.

As we celebrate Jubilee Dallas, I am proud to present, *Dallas Spirit.*

--- ❖ ---

INTRODUCTION

The drive from D/FW airport into downtown Dallas is exciting and even breathtaking — especially in the spring when fields of bluebonnets greet the visitor as he passes Texas Stadium, the home of the Dallas Cowboys. Driving on, he sees The University of Texas Southwestern Medical Center, which includes one of the most renowned medical schools in the country. Next, comes the Dallas Market Center complex, the only one of its kind in the nation. Looking ahead the visitor sees the aerial ball of Reunion Tower, the symbol which has become the Dallas Landmark. Behind it, majestic skyscrapers of steel and glass tower above the visitor. He knows he is entering a city of prosperity, innovation, and elegance.

Driving through the triple underpass, the gateway to the city, the visitor is startled by a tiny log cabin. This was the home of John Neely Bryan, the founder of Dallas.

The contrast of the log cabin and the skycrapers causes the visitor to wonder: "From these humble beginnings, how did Dallas develop into one of the ten power cities in the United States? It had to have been the creation of men and women with great vision!"

Who were these men and women with Dallas Spirit?

❖

DALLAS SPIRIT

When John Neely Bryan settled on the banks of the Trinity River in 1841, it was with the full intention of building a town. He had travelled from Arkansas to the Red River and then followed the trail known as "The Preston Road" to the banks of the Trinity River. Upon acquiring 640 acres from the Peters Colony, which was commissioned by the Republic of Texas to assign land to settlers, Bryan promptly sketched off a town designating a courthouse square and some 20 streets around it. He was already a real estate developer; he and an associate had made a success out of planning and selling the town of Van Buren, Arkansas. Real estate and land development were to weave through the political makeup of the city from this time forward.

Bryan persuaded settlers living farther down the river to move to his landing. He offered a free town lot to anyone who would join him. Among those he persuaded to relocate was the John Beeman family. Their daughter, Margaret, soon became his wife.

By 1843 there were enough people for the Republic of Texas to open postal service to the area, and John Neely Bryan became postmaster. Bryan named his town "Dallas," and the post office was housed in his log cabin home. How he arrived at the name "Dallas" will always remain a question. Several theories have been suggested, but none can be proven. Frank Cockrell, in his *Recollections,* quotes Bryan as saying "it was named for my friend Dallas." In June R. Welch's book, *Riding Fence,* Dr. Welch writes that Bryan's son informed an interviewer the town was named in honor of James K. Polk's vice-president, George Mifflin Dallas. In 1841, when the town was founded, George M. Dallas was a United States senator from Pennsylvania, and a leader for the future admission of Texas into the Union. Two years later, Polk and Dallas ran on an annexation platform. Writes Dr. Welch: "Those who argue that Dallas was not named for George Mifflin Dallas assume that Bryan could not have been aware of him; however, to anyone interested in Texas, Senator Dallas was anything but obscure when Bryan founded his town."

While Bryan was trying to attract more people to move into his village, other communities were springing up in the area. Across the Trinity River to the south, William Hord settled his 640-acre grant and called it "Hord's Ridge." This later became Oak Cliff. East of Dallas was a promising village called "Cedar Springs." To the north the most thriving of all the communities was "Farmer's Branch."

In 1845, the citizens of Texas voted to give up their independent republic status and be annexed by the United States. Dallas' official vote count was 29-3 in favor of annexation. To provide more efficient·local government, the first Texas State Legislature in 1846 created counties. All of the communities near the Trinity vied for the county seat. However, Dallas' dynamic leader, Bryan, won the important county seat and his log cabin became the first Dallas County Courthouse. John Neely Bryan was appointed county commissioner to organize the county which would encompass thirty miles. Soon, a large log cabin courthouse was constructed on the square (where the "Old Red" courthouse stands today).

Bryan was a man of vision with a trained legal mind. He was the prototype, in many ways, of the business and civic leaders who were to dominate the subsequent history of his city.

J. Wellington Latimer, hearing of the successful little town on the Trinity moved from Paris, Texas to Dallas in 1849. He started the first newspaper called the *Herald*. Unfortunately, Latimer was killed in a fall in 1859. His partner, J.W. Swindell, took over the paper and became very active in civic affairs. It remained the only major newspaper for almost twenty-five years.

While Bryan continued to be the driving force in the community, his good friend, Alexander Cockrell, was very instrumental in the original organization of the town. After he had settled 640 acres at Mountain Creek, west of Dallas, he bought all the remaining land that Bryan had for sale. In 1852, he and his wife built the first mansion in Dallas.

Cockrell operated a ferry which crossed the Trinity River. He built the first hotel, the Crutchfield House, on the courthouse square where the present Dealey Plaza is located. Shops were built around the square, and Dallas became a bustling little town. The Art Saloon on the south side of the square was a picture gallery and studio of Monsieur Gouhenant, a Frenchman who taught art and music. Another Frenchman, Maxime Guillot, opened a carriage factory in 1852. This first factory in Dallas built prized carriages for over fifty years. Other Frenchmen came to Dallas from the La Reunion colony farther down the Trinity and brought their culture to the village. No wonder that Dallas has become such an international center for the arts, with the early intellectual and artistic influence of the French.

Under the drive of Bryan and Cockrell, Dallas began to be noticed on the map of Texas. The two of them decided it was time to incorporate the town of 600 people. The State Legislature granted a charter on February 2, 1856.

On April 5, Samuel B. Pryor, a physician, was elected the first mayor of Dallas. Bryan and Cockrell served as two of six aldermen. An exciting event for Dallas that year was the completion of the first brick courthouse. Built in the center of the square, it was the pride of all the county.

John M. Crockett, an attorney and brother-in-law of William Hord, was elected mayor in 1857. Crockett, who had helped Bryan and Cockrell get the town incorporated, was, in effect, the first city attorney of Dallas.

In 1858, the town's leading industrialist and Bryan's best friend, Alexander Cockrell, was assassinated on a Dallas street by a disgruntled employee. The management of his large estate fell to his widow, Sarah, who expanded it with remarkable skill. Sarah Cockrell became the first capitalist of Dallas. Her enterprises would in time include an iron toll bridge across the Trinity River, the town's first major hotel, and seven or eight other profitable ventures. The opening of her St. Nicholas Hotel in 1859 was the biggest social event Dallas had ever seen. Its magnificent lobby featured a many-tiered chandelier and a spacious stairway· which led to the mezzanine.

By 1860, the town's official census was 775 persons. On July 8 of that same year, during a sleepy Sunday afternoon, a major tragedy struck. A fire began on the town square and spread quickly. It destroyed practically every building around the square including the St. Nicholas Hotel, the Crutchfield House, and most of the stores. The courthouse in the middle of the square survived, but it was badly damaged. No one knows for sure what caused the fire, but the abolitionists and Negroes wanting freedom were blamed. Some of the townspeople went beserk and beat a "confession" out of one of the Negroes. Three unpopular Negroes were hung on the square for the crime. However, many Dallas citizens did not believe the victims were guilty. The people of Dallas rebuilt their town around the square and most of the new structures were brick instead of frame.

Abraham Lincoln's election as President of the United States resulted in the withdrawl of Texas from the Union on February 23, 1861. Dallas citizens voted overwhelmingly in favor of secession. During the Civil War which followed, many of the citizens of Dallas fought on the side of the Confederate Army, including the town's first mayor, Dr. Samuel Pryor, who was killed in the war.

According to *The History of Dallas,* written by John Henry Brown, there had been no election for mayor during the Civil War. Crockett very well could have remained the mayor during this time as there is evidence that he was presiding in 1865 and 1866.

At the close of the Civil War in 1865, ex-confederates flocked to Dallas from other parts of the former Confederacy. Not only were the followers of Robert E. Lee and Jefferson Davis arriving, but veterans who had followed Grant and Lincoln also came to make their home in the prospering town. Putting aside their division of sentiment, the "Yanks" and the "Men from Dixie" united and the Dallas Spirit of non-partisanship, in all matters affecting the vital interest of their home community, was born. The leadership of Dallas soon was composed of such historical names as Captain W.H. Gaston, Colonel C.C. Slaughter and General W.L. Cabell.

Many of the former slaves stayed in Dallas after they were freed. The black people formed a community in the northern part of the city around Hall and Washington Streets. Since desegregation in the 1950s, Blacks live throughout the city. Many Blacks live in the southern part of Dallas (Oak Cliff); however, the original north Dallas area is still a thriving Black community. Today, African-Americans are active in all aspects of the city's development. In 1969, George Allen was the first Black to be elected to the Dallas City Council. He was followed by such notables as Fred Blair, Lucy Patterson, Elsie Faye Heggins, Juanita Craft, Al Lipscomb, and Diane Ragsdale. Activists Pettis Norman, Marvin Crenshaw, Roy Williams, and Dallas County Commissioner John Wiley Price have raised the political consciousness of Dallas. Religious leaders S.M. Wright and Zan Holmes are voices that speak to all Dallasites. Country western great Charlie Pride is a renowned banker. Marvin Robinson and Comer Cottrell, a member of the elite Citizens Council, have opened new doors of business opportunities. Dallas is fortunate to have the leadership and dedication of its African Americans.

After the Civil War, the defeated southern states were under military rule with General Philip Sheridan in command. This military government appointed mayors to the cities. In September 1868, Ben Long, a native of Switzerland and a devoted unionist, was appointed mayor of Dallas. Long resigned on April 1, 1870, to travel to his native land. A newly-installed regime in Austin, headed by Edmund J. Davis, appointed Henry S. Ervay as Long's successor. Ervay accepted, but only "after due deliberation." He did so "not only with the consent but also upon the urgent solicitation of the best people in town, irrespective of party feeling," as stated in Sam Acheson's book *Dallas Yesterday*.

It was during Ervay's term in 1871, that Dallas was incorporated as a city . This enlarged its city limits to one and one half square miles. Mayor Ervay and his fellow aldermen were at the center of moves to ensure Dallas' entry into the railroad age. In 1871 and 1872, the people of Dallas voted for cash subsidies to both the Houston-Central and the Texas-Pacific railroads. The art of political persuasion, which was to become a hallmark of Dallas development and prosperity, was exercised at its best by Alderman W.H. Gaston. In order to assure future development, he generously donated right-of-way through his land, as well as property for the Union Depot, which was located at what is now the intersection of Pacific and Central Expressway. The first passenger train, the Houston-Central, arrived in Dallas July 16, 1872. John Neely Bryan sat on the platform as the townspeople celebrated with speeches and a picnic. Indeed it was a great day in Dallas. On February 22, 1873, when the Texas-Pacific train came in from the east, Dallas was on its way to greatness! Dallas became the first railroad crossroads town in Texas.

The happy occasion of the arrival of the first train in Dallas seems to be the last reported event that John Neely Bryan attended. According to Lucy C. Trent, in her book, *John Neely Bryan: Founder of Dallas*, the Bryan family had moved to the original Cockrell home in Mountain Creek. Sometime in the mid-1870s, Bryan entered the State Hospital for Nervous Diseases in Austin and died there in 1877. Frank X. Tolbert wrote later in *The Dallas Morning News* that Bryan's mind got "clouded" toward the end of his life. No one seems to know where John Neely Bryan's grave is located, but certainly his log cabin in downtown Dallas is a shrine to the great man of spirit who founded our city.

By 1872, the new government in Austin allowed local elections. Upon his return from Switzerland, Ben Long was elected mayor. The two years of Long's second term, with Aldermen G.W. Swink, C. Copy, M. Thevenet, Captain W.H. Gaston, Arch M. Cochran and J.W. Long, were critical ones in the transformation of the frontier hamlet into an expanding and prospering city. There is no question that the crossing of the north-south and east-west railroads is what made Dallas, the frontier town, boom into Dallas, the metropolitan center. By the end of 1873, Dallas had a new $75,000 courthouse located at Akard and Commerce. The effect of the town's first railroads, the Houston and Texas Central in 1872, and the Texas and Pacific in 1873, would increase the population from less than 2,500 to more than 7,000 in a matter of months.

Where trade routes intersect, men inevitably meet to barter the products of the region. The combination of the railroads and cotton grown in the area made Dallas eventually become the cotton capital of the world. At first the cotton traders filled the streets until the Gaston Building was built to house them. In 1925, the Cotton Exchange Building was built and foreign cotton merchants came from all over the world to settle here. Certainly cotton was the agricultural product that first brought Dallas world prominence.

Immediately after the cotton boom began, financial

institutions arose. Gaston opened the first bank which became the First National Bank of Dallas and later The First International Bank.

The Board of Aldermen during Ben Long's second administration, and Dallas' first heyday, was a good cross section of pre-Civil War leadership. The newcomers did not immediately assert themselves in the area of politics; therefore, there was not a rush of new blood in the civic and business leadership of Dallas.

Dallas attracted many different businesses and industries. This diversity kept Dallas prosperous years later when other cities were having economic slumps.

In 1872, Alex Sanger, a merchant from Corsicana, and his brother, Philip, built a store which became the largest mercantile business in North Texas. Sanger Brothers became known nationally and the fashion industry was born in Dallas because of the vision of these two brothers. The original Sanger Brothers store was located where El Centro College stands today. Although many other good and successful stores opened, such as A. Harris and Titche Goettinger, Sanger Brothers monopolized the entire mercantile business for nearly fifty years. Alex Sanger died in 1925 (his brother Philip had died in 1902). A few years later the Sanger Brothers store was sold to a company in Kansas City. Herbert Marcus, a former Sanger Brothers employee, his sister Carrie, an A. Harris employee, and Carrie's husband Al Neiman started their specialty store, Neiman-Marcus in 1907. When the new Sanger Brothers owners released fifty employees from salespeople to seamstresses, Neiman-Marcus hired them all. The customers moved with their favorite salespeople. This was the turning point for Neiman-Marcus according to Stanley Marcus in *The Book of Dallas*. Neiman-Marcus made Dallas the "fashion center of the world."

The moral well-being of the community took priority in the second Long administration. With so many people moving in, preventing vice and immorality was of utmost importance. Closely allied with the moral well-being of the city was the physical well-being, and the first city hospital opened in 1873. The Board of Aldermen gave a franchise to the City Railroad Company to operate horse or mule-drawn streetcars on Main Street between the courthouse and the railroad depot. The Coal Gasworks of James S. Hamilton, which used artificial gas extracted from coal, lighted the streets and homes.

The next city election in 1874 saw many newcomers emerge into prominent leadership roles. Former Confederate General and West Point graduate W.L. Cabell, a two-year resident, defeated Long for reelection by a vote of 740-522. The Board of Aldermen had a number of completely new faces including Alex Sanger, William G. Sterrett, a newspaperman, and the Reverand William C. Young, a minister of the First Methodist Church. Alderman Sanger led the move whereby the Board of Aldermen met in the comfortable chambers of the new Dallas Commercial Club, forerunner of the Dallas Chamber of Commerce.

The Constitution of Texas, in 1875, authorized incorporated cities to provide free education to all children and to levy a school tax. Acting on this authority, the city council, under Mayor Cabell's vigorous leadership, held elections, voted taxes, and passed an ordinance organizing and governing the city's free public schools. Teachers' certificates were signed by the mayor and the city council appointed four trustees, one for each ward of the city. The selection of school sites became an immediate activity of the city council.

Southwestern Life Insurance Company was started in

Dallas in 1876 and Dallas was to become the most important insurance center in the state.

One of the most shocking events in the early history of Dallas happened in 1877. Former Mayor Ben Long was in a beer saloon at Austin and Wood Streets when two men and a woman started to leave without paying. Long intervened and one of the men shot and killed him. Mayor Cabell visited the scene of the crime in the course of an official investigation. Cabell, who had defeated Long for mayor, personally led a posse and the assassin was killed trying to cross the Trinity River.

During the 1870's, many churches were built. St. Matthews Episcopal Church, and Temple Emanu-El went up on Commerce Street. Several protestant churches were contructed including Baptist, Presbyterian, and Methodist. Sacred Heart Catholic Church was built in 1874 and twenty years later, in 1894, under the direction of Bishop E.J. Dunne, the beautiful Cathedral of the Sacred Heart was erected on Ross Avenue. Today it is the Cathedral of Our Lady of Guadalupe. In 1874, the Catholic order of Ursuline nuns opened an academy in a majestic gothic structure on Bryan Street. Today, over 100 years later, Ursuline Academy, located on Walnut Hill Lane, is still considered one of the finest girls' schools in the state. In December 1879, on the eastern outskirts of Dallas, the Reverend R.C. Buckner established Buckner's Orphans Home using John Neely Bryan's original cabin as one of his first buildings. Although he was a Baptist minister, the home was open to children of all faiths.

In 1880, Dr. J.W. Crowdus became mayor. He had been president of Sarah Cockrell's Dallas Bridge Company which built the iron bridge over the Trinity River. During his term as mayor, the city's first telephone line connected the water plant at Browder Springs with the fire station at Commerce and Lamar.

W.L. Cabell took the mayor's chair again in 1882. The effective leadership of the former mayor provided the first electric plant to be operated in Dallas and the first sewer lines to be installed in downtown Dallas.

Future historian and writer, John Henry Brown, was elected mayor in 1884 and was instrumental in forming a separate School Board of Education.

Colonel A.H. Belo, who ran a very successful newspaper in Galveston, learned of the rapidly growing town in north Texas and sent his right-hand man, George Bannerman Dealey, to Dallas to scout the possibility of starting a newspaper. Dealey immediately felt that Dallas was the place to be, and the first edition of *The Dallas Morning News* came off the press October 1, 1885. William Sterrett, then owner of *The Herald*, sold his paper to Belo. However, because *The Herald* had been such a well known newspaper, Charles E. Gilbert used the name in 1888 when he started *The Dallas Times Herald*. The two newspapers remain the only dailies in Dallas today.

Colonel Belo moved his family to Dallas and the Belo Mansion still stands on Ross Avenue between Olive and Pearl Streets. It is now the Dallas Legal Education Center. After Colonel Belo's death in 1901, Vice-President and General Manager George Dealey took complete charge of the operations of *The Dallas Morning News*. In 1926, Dealey bought the newspaper and George Bannerman Dealey became one of the most respected and visionary men in Dallas history. He was followed with the same spirit by his son Ted, and grandson Joe, who made *The Dallas Morning News* one of the leading newspapers in the country. Its influence was enormous, and represented the dominant voice of Dallas. The Dealey name is synonymous with Dallas spirit and George Bannerman Dealey's statue is proudly displayed in Dealey Plaza, the original town square, across from the Old Red Courthouse. Today, as chairman of the board of the A.H. Belo Corporation, the parent company of *The Dallas Morning News*, Robert W. Decherd continues the legacy of dedication and vision of his great-grandfather, George Bannerman Dealey.

In the early 1880s, a figure well outside the usual mold of Dallas politicians emerged. Winship C. (Bud) Connor, at the age of twenty-four, had organized the city's first volunteer fire department in 1873 and became its first unpaid chief. He was later given the city's second telephone so he could call the waterworks at Browder Springs for more pressure should a fire occur. During his tenure as chief, Dallas acquired its first steam fire engine, "Ol' Tige," now the pride of the Dallas Fire Museum.

Conner met the criteria for civic energy and aggressiveness, but he was also known for his flashy dress and flambouyant manner. He organized the first Dallas waterworks and sold it to the city in 1881 after cutting off the fire station and the hospital during a fuss with aldermen over municipal bills. In 1883, he became president of the city's first electric company.

In 1887, Connor decided he was ready to try to unseat the incumbent mayor, John Henry Brown. Another candidate was Ed Smith, a popular funeral director. By this time, Connor had come to be considered the favorite of the so-called "liberal element," and he won by only three votes after a hotly contested race.

In this same year, under Connor's leadership, the State Fair of Texas was established. This began a long and successful history as a major exposition. It has always received the support of the ablest and busiest leaders of Dallas.

Dallas joined the newly organized Texas Baseball League in 1887, and in 1888, in its first season, the Dallas Tigers won the pennant. T.L. Marsalis, an investor in Hord's Ridge (Oak Cliff) built a railway line from Dallas' courthouse square, over an elevated trestle, crossing the Trinity River to the ballpark. This railway line was ready for opening day, April 22, 1888, and its modern coaches carried baseball fans to the park. The ballpark remained in the same place next to the Trinity River in Oak Cliff, and later streetcars took fans across the viaduct. The team changed names several times from the Tigers, to the Steers, to the Rebels, and finally to the Eagles, and Dallas fans always remained loyal. Instrumental in making baseball the star attraction in Dallas through the long and prosperous regime of the Texas League were such personalities as Julius and George Schepps, Dick Burnett, and Bobby Goff. Goff brought nine major league old-time greats to Dallas including Ty Cobb, Tris Speaker, Dizzy and Paul Dean, and Mickey Cochran, to open the 1950 season in the Cotton Bowl. This game still holds the attendance record of any baseball game in Texas with 53,758. Baseball was certainly "America's favorite pastime" in Dallas for over fifty years. The combined region made up of Ft. Worth, Arlington, and Dallas, joined forces to bring major league baseball to the area in 1972. The three mayors, R.M. Stovall of Ft. Worth, Tommy Vandergriff of Arlington, and Wes Wise of Dallas, convinced the major league owners to allow Bob Short, owner of the Washington Senators, to move his American League franchise to Texas. The team was named the Texas Rangers. In 1974, Short sold the Rangers to a group of prominent local businessmen.

Today, the Texas Rangers are owned by George W. Bush, son of the President of the United States and Ed "Rusty" Rose.

In 1889, the more staid and "conservative" voters were relieved when former mayor Cabell announced he would contest the colorful Connor. Ed Smith also ran again. But when the April 2, 1889 election was over, Connor had once again triumphed with 3,015 votes to Cabell's 1,584 and Smith's 387. During this term, electric streetcars were installed, replacing horse-drawn streetcars.

Connor used his best political skills to lead the way for annexation of East Dallas. In his dramatic manner, on New Year's Eve, December 31, 1889, he arrived at the East Dallas City Council Meeting and accepted transfer of that city to Dallas. On New Year's Day, January 1, 1890, with a population increased to 38,067, Dallas was assured first place in the 1890 census as the largest city in Texas. This was the first and only time that Dallas held this position.

Dallas from the earliest days was a town of culture, charm, and society. In the early 1880s, it had two theaters and a 1200 seat Dallas Opera House in which Edwin Booth, Lawrence Barrett, Maurice Barrymore, and Sarah Bernhardt performed. The Grand Windsor and the Le Grande hotels were the centers of social activities during the 1880s. The Idlewild Club was organized by Dallas bachelors to give the young ladies "coming out" in society a proper occasion to make their bow. Its first ball was held in 1884. In 1893, the grand dame of hotels, The Oriental, was built by Tom Field at Akard and Commerce streets. It was fully electrified including elevators. The Oriental was the undisputed social center of Dallas for the next twenty years.

The game of golf was introduced in Dallas before the turn of the century, and some of the most prominent men in the city established the Dallas Golf Club in 1897. They purchased thirty acres east of Oak Lawn at Lemmon Avenue on Turtle Creek, where high-rise condominiums are located today. They built an elegant clubhouse and golf course. In 1912, the club moved three miles up Turtle Creek to Highland Park, and its name was changed to the Dallas Country Club.

In 1891, both the Democratic and Republican parties decided to run candidates against Mayor Bud Conner. The Democrats ran George Cole from a well-known pioneer family, and the Republicans ran a man named Brownlee. Conner won again with a vote of 4,347 to Cole's 3,571, and 29 votes for Brownlee.

The famous landmark courthouse, "Old Red," was completed in the center of John Neely Bryan's original square in 1891, and remained the active Dallas County Courthouse until the 1960s. "Old Red," along with Bryan's cabin, are the most sentimental landmarks in Dallas today.

In 1893, Conner sought a fourth term. His opponent, Bryan T. Barry, was a leading member of the Dallas bar. Barry, a former state legislator and former chairman of the Texas State Democratic Party, lost to Conner by two votes. Barry filed a complaint and lost the decision in the lower district court in Dallas. However, in 1894, the Texas Supreme Court reversed the lower court decision and declared Barry mayor.

Barry presided over meetings in Dallas' first impressive city hall, a five-story building which cost $500,000. It was located at Commerce and Akard streets.

While Connor is associated with the start of the city's water distribution system, Barry is credited with having initiated the surface reservoirs which furnished the chief source of city water. The two reservoirs, created by the Barry administration, were located behind dams built on the Elm Fork of the Trinity River at Record Crossing and California streets.

The new county-owned Parkland Hospital was opened on the outskirts of the city at Maple and Oak Lawn in 1894, and St. Paul Hospital, a Roman Catholic institution staffed by the Daughters of Charity nuns, opened east of downtown in 1898. The First Baptist Church was built at Ervay and San Jacinto streets that same year. It was to become the largest Baptist congregation in the world and Baptists still worship at the same location today.

In 1895, Colonel Frank P. Holland, an alderman since 1891 and publisher of *Farm and Ranch* magazine, and A. P. Wozencraft, former Adjutant General of Texas, decided to challenge Barry for mayor. Holland won by 60 votes.

Holland was a long-time chairman of the Trinity River Navigation Committee of the Dallas Chamber of Commerce, and was one of the organizers and later a director of the State Fair of Texas.

In 1898, John H. Traylor became mayor. Not much is known about his administration.

Dallas began the twentieth century with a population of 42,638. It had become a big city, but the unique character of Dallas' citizens kept it more like a small town. Everyone seemed to know everyone else. People gathered at the Oriental Hotel for social functions, rode the streetcar across the viaduct to watch their baseball team, and *all* of the people were concerned with their city. There was a joyous sense of community spirit and a real pride that made everyone feel a part of this wonderful town.

On April 13, 1900, Ben E. Cabell, son of the former Mayor W. L. Cabell, became mayor for two terms. During his first term, a city-owned public library opened at Commerce and Harwood streets and the city-sponsored Dallas Symphony Orchestra gave its first concert. The first University of Dallas, a Catholic college, was opened in 1900 on Oak Lawn Avenue, where the Turtle Creek Village stands today. The University of Dallas is now located in Irving and is one of the most respected academic institutions in the country. The first electric interurban line provided hourly service between Fort Worth and Dallas in 1902 and shortly thereafter regular service was established to Denison, Sherman, Terrell, Waco, and Ennis. Dallas was the center of this interurban network. During his second term, Mayor Cabell also began efforts for Oak Cliff to merge with Dallas.

Dallas hosted the United Confederate Veterans convention in April 1902 and the city went all out to receive three to four thousand former soldiers. The Civil War had ended nearly four decades before. Most of the "rebels" were well along in years, the majority of them sixty or seventy years of age or older. The patriotic citizens of Dallas opened their spare bedrooms, their attics, and their basements for the visitors at no charge. Texas had fought under the flag of the Confederacy and the people of Dallas were determined to honor the men from Dixie in a deserving manner.

In 1904, former Mayor Bryan T. Barry was elected mayor again and his administration started the park system. Soon Oak Lawn Park (now Lee Park) opened at Lemmon and Turtle Creek adjacent to the Dallas Golf Club. Farther west, down the creek at Maple, a larger park opened in 1914 called Reverchon, named for a La Reunion naturalist. Baseball diamonds were installed and the semi-pro ballplayers held games there. It was also during Barry's administration that Oak Cliff residents approved annexation by Dallas, a movement started by Cabell.

Curtis T. Smith's administration, beginning in 1906, chalked up an admirable record. He was responsible for extensive brick paving on downtown thoroughfares and the first vehicle traffic ordinance was passed. The ordinance required a license number on every vehicle and a horn or bell to give warning of its approach.

Some of the leaders of Dallas became dissatisfied with the aldermanic form of government. In 1907, Henry D. Lindsley formed a group known as the Citizens Association. Their purpose was to replace the fourteen-man Board of Aldermen with a commission form of government. The association's driving force came from 100 of the town's "top brass" including bankers Royal A. Ferris and J. B. Wilson and other leaders such as C. Weichel, George Loudermilk and George Leachman. Their goal was to "interest the public service to businessmen upon their pledge to conduct it according to business principles and to have a non-political government."

The new charter, approved by the Texas State Legislature, was adopted on April 9, 1907. It called for a mayor and four commissioners who would be in charge of fire and police, water, streets and finance. The Citizens Association slate, led by mayoralty candidate Stephen J. Hay, won overwhelmingly. The commission form of government was considered by the majority of citizens to be a marked advancement over the aldermanic system.

The four years of the S.J. Hay administration witnessed unusual growth and prosperity for Dallas. An "adequate" water supply for all time — it was thought — was in sight as White Rock Dam and Lake neared completion on the northeastern outskirts of Dallas.

The city's first skyscraper, the fourteen-story Praetorian (Insurance) Building, at the corner of Main and Stone Streets was built. Darwin Payne says in his book *Dallas; An Illustrated History* that, "Residents could go to the top floor for twenty-five cents and enjoy a grand, unimpeded view of the town such as they never before had seen."

The first automobile assembly plant in Texas opened in Dallas on December 17, 1909, and the citizens of Dallas eagerly waited to see the first car made in their city. That first car rolled off the assembly line in early January 1910. The automobile influenced the citizens of Dallas from the very beginning. Automobile dealers were to become some of the most civic-minded citizens in Dallas including Dr. G. Langley, Ed Maher, Earl Hayes, W.O. Bankston, and Rodger Meier.

The Adolphus Hotel opened in 1910 across the street from The Oriental. Built by Adolphus Busch, the beer magnate, the hotel was considered an architectural marvel, and remained one of Dallas' finest through the 1950s. Renovated in the 1980s, it is again one of the finest hotels in the city today.

At a cost of $700,000, the largest concrete bridge in the world was completed in 1912. The Oak Cliff (now Houston Street) viaduct was built high above the Trinity River connecting Dallas and Oak Cliff.

The first native son to be elected mayor of Dallas was thirty-six year old William Meredith Holland. He had been elected judge of the Dallas County Court at Law but resigned to run in the city election as nominee of the Citizens Association. In 1911, he began the first of two terms. During Holland's administration, Dallas secured a water treatment plant as well as a sewage pumping plant. His administration was also responsible for building Woodlawn Hospital, the first municipally-owned hospital for tuberculosis in the state. Baylor Baptist Memorial Sanitorium, predecessor to the Baylor University Medical Center, had opened the previous year.

By 1911, the Southern Methodists had agreed to locate a major university on the northern edge of town. This university, named Southern Methodist University (S.M.U.), was a major pride to Dallas and remains so today.

Dallas had become such an important banking center that when Congress passed the Federal Reserve Act of 1913, Dallas was named as location for one of twelve regional Federal Reserve Banks in the nation.

The new marble-halled five-million dollar city hall at Main, Harwood and Commerce streets, along with the skyscrapers surrounding it, showed the progress that had been made in the six years of administration by men selected by the Citizens Association. As sponsor of the commission plan, the men of the Citizens Association, with their foresight, were riding the crest of public esteem and popularity.

In 1915, Henry D. Lindsley, the founder of the Citizens Association, was elected mayor with a turnout of 12,859 of 15,963 qualified voters at the polls. This is believed to be the highest percentage turnout of any mayoral election in Dallas history.

During Lindsley's terms, the Union Railway Station was completed. The building cost five million dollars and the railroads were all rerouted to go to this magnificent terminal on Houston Street.

By 1917, when Lindsley was up for reelection, his opponents, who proclaimed themselves to be apostles of the old line conservatism, charged him with creating a number of useless city agencies. Two of his pet projects were a City Board of Public Health and a City Department for Public Welfare. Under heavy fire were the Free Legal Aid Bureau, the City Employment Office, the Reorganization of Parkland City Hospital, and the establishment of an overnight shelter for what today would be known as "street or homeless people." The predominant issue, however, centered around a controversy about new public utility franchises, which Lindsley opposed. The older generation of Citizens Association members, such as Royal Ferris, E.O. Tennison, and J.B. Wilson, stuck loyally to the C.A. ticket. However, others, such as Sam Cochran, Edgar Flippen, Eli Sanger, and Dr. E.H. Cary, supported Joe E. Lawther for mayor. Lawther defeated Lindsley, but all other Citizens Association candidates won. Lawther's victory marked the first time any Citizens Association candidate had lost since the start of the commission form of government.

The United States had become involved in World War I, and the State Fair grounds became Camp Dick, an army training post for aviator candidates. A training base for the United States Air Force was opened on a field north of Dallas and was called Love Field. After the war, Love Field was given to the city for a municipal field. Charles A. Lindbergh landed his famous "Spirit of St. Louis" airplane at Love Field for the dedication of the airport. An estimated 100,000 people cheered the popular aviator as he rode in a parade through downtown Dallas. First passenger service began in 1928 by Texas Air Transport (now American Airlines) with service to Houston and San Antonio.

Frank W. Wozencraft, only 26 when he returned from the service in World War I, headed the Citizens Association ticket in 1919. Incumbent Mayor Joe Lawther headed a slate known as the Good Government Association to oppose Wozencraft and the Citizens Association. The Democratic Party decided to endorse the Citizens Association slate and they won overwhelmingly.

After the war, Dallas was booming and Mayor Wozencraft's administration produced many achievements. The First National Bank Building and the Magnolia Petroleum Building, a towering 29-story edifice, rose to dominate the local skyline. This building, known fondly to many as the "tall one with the flying red horse on top," was a popular way for travellers to know they were getting close to Dallas. The Magnolia Building remained Dallas' tallest skyscraper for over twenty-five years. The merchants, who had earlier organized a semi-annual southwestern fashion show for retailers, opened a Dallas downtown market center. This market place was the predecessor of today's giant Dallas Market Center complex on Stemmons Freeway.

Dallas was truly a place of contentment during the post-World War I years. The conservative atmosphere put family, religion, and the good of the community first. Honesty and morality were commonplace and a handshake was all that was needed for a business deal or money loaned.

Citizens regularly went downtown to the theater district on Elm Street for entertainment. The magnificent Majestic and Palace theaters showed the popular movies of the day. Often the stars came in person for the openings of the "picture shows." Karl St. John Hoblitzelle, who had come to Dallas in 1903 with his Interstate Amusement Company featuring vaudeville, developed and operated the city's movie chain. Hoblitzelle became chairman of the board of the Republic National Bank. He acquired many other business ventures and became one of the wealthiest men in the city. During his life he was a

leader in Dallas' development. His philanthropic generosity is still felt throughout the city today.

Looking ahead, Mayor Wozencraft called for the re-
moval of the Houston and Texas Central railroad tracks,
which later became Central Expressway.

1919 was the year that women could vote at last.
Mayor Wozencraft formed a committee of women leaders to probe the high cost of ice. The Dallas House-
wives Chamber of Commerce commended the mayor
for the establishment of another committee to combat
rent profiteering resulting from the shortage of post-war
housing.

The city of Dallas honored World War I General John
J. Pershing on February 7, 1920. Riding in the parade
with Mayor Wozencraft, the general turned to him and
exclaimed, "What a City! Such vitality and exuberance!"

Wozencraft was considered so outstanding in his office that sixty-four mayors meeting in Dallas proposed
that he be named governor of Texas. However, the
mayor reminded them that he was under the legal age
limit of 30 to be governor. Wozencraft refused to run
for reelection as mayor stating, "I have spent two years
in army service and two more in public service. It is
imperative that I return to private practice." Just ten
years later the still young attorney became general coun-
sel for the Radio Corporation of America (RCA) in New
York City.

The early 1920s brought out the Ku Klux Klan in full
force. Dallas' chapter was said to be the largest in the
state. The imperial wizard of the national Klan, Dr.
Hiram Wesley Evans, was a Dallas dentist. Klansmen
paraded in full regalia, burned crosses, flogged Blacks,
and attempted to run Jews and Catholics out of town.
These horrendous activities went on far too long, with

the law enforcement officials ignoring and some even seeming to condone the Klan's inhumanity. *The Dallas Morning News*, however, bravely opposed KKK activities. A group of anti-Klan businessmen organized the Dallas County Citizens League to rid the city of this menacing band of bigots and they succeeded. The Citizens Association, in 1921, turned to Sawnie R. Aldredge to run for mayor and he won handily. Zoning and planning for the city began to take shape during his administration as Ed A. Wood was hired to carry out the master plan established a decade before.

In May 1921, the first radio station, WRR, 1310 on the dial, began broadcasting. The studio was located in the Jefferson Hotel across from Union Station. The radio station continues today as KAAM, 1310 on the AM dial.

In 1922, the Junior League of Dallas received its charter from the Association of Junior Leagues of America. Their record of humanitarian services is unsurpassed. Today, the Junior League's dedicated women continue to administer to practically every major cause in the city. Women's influence was beginning to be recognized through other organizations as well. Through the years, the women of Dallas have been instrumental in raising funds for charities, the arts, civic improvements, medical research, beautification projects, as well as personal volunteering. Some of the most prominent women of Dallas, who have given time, money, and talents are Ruth Sharp Altshuler, Lindalyn Adams, Nancy Hamon, Carla Francis, Nancy Brinker, Margot Perot, and Margaret McDermott. Dallas women who are movers and shakers in the business world include Mary Kay Ash, Ebby Halliday, and Caroline Rose Hunt. Women who opened doors for other women worked within the political arena. Such instrumental women include Calvert

Collins, Elizabeth Blessing, Anita Martinez, Adlene Harrison, Lori Palmer, and Eddie Bernice Johnson.

In 1923, Louis W. Blaylock, the publisher of *The Texas Christian Advocate,* who had served as mayor pro tem and Commissioner of Finance under Aldredge, won overwhelmingly as the Citizens Association candidate for mayor. In 1925, he was reelected and swept the entire C.A. slate into office with him.

During this time, new landscaping was developed where John Neely Bryan's original square had been. A lovely park faced the "Old Red" courthouse which was later named Dealey Plaza after the founders of *The Dallas Morning News.* The Baker Hotel was built where The Oriental once stood. Its grand opening was held on October 9, 1926. The magnificent Baker shared honors with the Adolphus across the street as the centers of Dallas social events through the 1950s.

The Hispanic community increased in Dallas between 1925 and 1930, settling in an area northwest of downtown known as "Little Mexico." Today, Little Mexico is still a concentrated hispanic area, but many Hispanics are located throughout the city bringing to Dallas a culture rich in tradition. Annually, the hispanic community celebrates Cinco de Mayo, in honor of their independence. The entire city joins in the festivities which features mariachi bands, bright-colored decorations and costumes, and some of the best food in the Southwest. The Hispanic influence has helped make Dallas a cosmopolitan city. Spanish is spoken throughout the area. Notable members of the Hispanic community include Anita Martinez who was elected to the city council in 1969, followed by Pedro Aguirre, Ricardo Medrano and Al Gonzales. Adelfa Callejo, an attorney, has been a leader among the Hispanic activists in Dallas. No names are better known throughout the city than restaurateurs Pete Dominguez, the Cuellar family, and Martinez family. The Highland Park Village, the oldest shopping center in the Southwest, owes its architectural design to the Hispanic culture, as does the Casa Linda Shopping Center. Many of the historic homes along Swiss Avenue reflect the same architectural style. The Spirit of Dallas is reflected in the many contributions of the Hispanic community.

By 1927 the city had grown to a population of 260,000 and the commission form of government had become a disappointment to many of the business and civic leaders. A group of non-partisan candidates favored the council-manager form of government. The mayoral candidate, Robert E. Burt, if elected, promised to appoint a committee to work out the details for a submission to the people of Dallas. He was elected in a runoff with John C. Harris who had been mayor pro tem and commissioner of finance in the previous administration.

Burt came through on his promise and appointed a committee of fifteen outstanding citizens to draft a new city charter which would embody a new city manager plan. A former city attorney, Hugh S. Grady, was named committee chairman. The main job of drafting a new charter was assigned to a subcommittee including Grady, another former city attorney, Charles F. O'Donnell, and Louis P. Head, the long-time staff specialist on municipal affairs at *The Dallas Morning News*. This monumental task would take twenty-three months to complete.

In the meantime came the 1929 election, often described as the wildest in Dallas' history. J. Worthington (Waddy) Tate, who had been defeated in the previous election, ran a strong populist campaign. He promised donkeys in the park, a Coney Island at White Rock Lake, and free telephones for stranded motorists on the Houston Street Viaduct. Tate called his followers the "blue shirt boys." He was known for being a flambouyant dresser and carried a gold-headed cane. Tate promised to call a charter election if elected, and he won in a runoff.

Tate, who became known as the "hot dog mayor," and was referred to by *Time* magazine as "The Hickory-Cured Mayor of Dallas," refused to call a charter election. The late H.P. Kucera, then assistant city attorney, said in the Dallas Mayors Oral History Project: "...So the citizens became sort of aroused about this and the Citizens Charter group proceeded to go ahead and get petitions for an initiated referendum and they got more signatures and this mayor still wouldn't call the election, but he had to — he was compelled by the court to do that." So, an election was held on October 10, 1930, and the city-manager form of government was approved by the voters 2-to-1. Citizens were to vote for their nine-member council early in April and the new charter would go into effect May 1, 1931.

The Citizens Association that had begun in 1907 had been organized with the idea of drafting outstanding citizens to govern the city in a businesslike manner, and change the system of government from Dallas' original aldermanic system to commissioner form. Some twenty years later, many of these same citizens were the ones dissatisfied with the commissioner form and favored the council-manager system. This system would elect nine members at large, with the newly elected council selecting one of themselves to be mayor.

Their idea of selecting businessmen to govern the city as a business did not change. However, the newly formed Citizens Charter Association (C.C.A.) went even further in the selectiveness of the candidates. Its famous quote was "the office seeking the candidate, not the candidate seeking the office." Thus, no one dared go to the top leaders and offer their services. To "want" the position appeared to be political and the C.C.A. did not want "politicians" in the city government in Dallas. Therefore, "politics" only occurred within the C.C.A. itself.

The C.C.A. had little opposition in the first election of the council-manager form of government on April 6, 1931, and the entire slate won overwhelmingly. T.L. Bradford was selected unanimously by the council to be mayor.

Bradford, the board chairman of Southwestern Life Insurance Company, had been a former partner of Ashley Cullum in the grocery business. He had taken over the small insurance company in 1912 and developed it into one of the largest in the southwest. Having purchased the property that had once been the frontier town of Cedar Springs, he built his own mansion and a hospital for babies in memory of his first wife and their deceased daughter. The C.C.A. felt that Bradford was the ideal man to be the "chairman of the board" of the council.

Bradford immediately plunged into the overhaul of the city hall. He worked closely with the first city manager, John N. Edy, redeveloping the government of Dallas. At the same time, he continued to run his insurance company.

Mayor Bradford was very well liked, and his generosity and aggressive but amiable demeanor made the transition go smoothly. Dallas was thriving under Bradford when tragedy struck.

On August 22, 1932, the mayor was chatting with a group of friends in the clubroom of the City Club, then located in the Southland Building next door to the Baker

Hotel, when he was stricken with a massive heart attack and died. His death was a great shock to Dallas.

Mayor Pro Tem, Charles E. Turner, immediately became mayor after the unexpected death of Mayor Bradford. A native Dallasite, Turner had served in the army during World War I and was a salesman for a wholesale drug company in Dallas. He became mayor at the beginning of the Great Depression.

The diversity of Dallas' commercial and industrial businesses prevented the city from suffering the grave situations that the "Great Depression" caused throughout the country. In addition, the East Texas Field, the oil boom in east Texas, brought more business to Dallas because Dallas was a financial center. Some of the most successful oil operators, such as H.L. Hunt and Everette Lee DeGolyer, made their headquarters and homes in Dallas.

However, by the fall of 1932, unemployment in Dallas had reached crisis proportions, and the city opened soup kitchens and administered relief to the needy. Though the cost was enormous, Mayor Turner and the council initially refused federal assistance. Finally, with the urging of the Community Chest and the Chamber of Commerce, Dallas accepted a government loan.

Having seen how much federal loans could help, the next year Turner led a fight to use federal aid for highway improvements.

Mayor Turner worked diligently with the leaders of Dallas to obtain the Texas Centennial Celebration which was upcoming in 1936. One city was to be designated as the site for the official state-wide centennial observance, and all of the major cities were vying for this honor. Mayor Turner, along with banker Fred Florence, drew up the city's formal bid. R.L. Thornton, a prominent banker and president of the Chamber of Commerce, directed the Dallas campaign which was competing with San Antonio and Houston. Quoting C.C.A. leader John Stemmons in his Mayors Oral History Project, "It all started in 1935 by Mr. R.L. Thornton, who said, 'I want 100 of you damn fellows to be at my beck and call, and I want you to be able to say 'yes' or 'no' when there's something that I want you to do.' And they said 'yes' to get the Centennial Exposition, and that's the way the Citizens Council started." They enlisted the Work Projects Administration, (WPA), to build the triple underpass for the railroads over Elm, Commerce and Main streets as the gateway to the city which led to the Centennial grounds (now Fair Park). The WPA, the federal agency charged with initiating and administering public works in order to relieve national unemployment, also built many of the Exposition Buildings at the park.

"Mr. Turner has made Dallas a good mayor in a particularly difficult period in the city's development," *The Dallas Journal* commented when Turner announced that he would not seek reelection. Instead, Turner joined the Centennial executive staff as director of finance and shaped the brillant spectacle called "The Cavalcade of Texas." On March 5, 1936, just three months before the Centennial opened, Mayor Turner was stricken with a heart attack and died. "The Cavalcade" became a tribute to him.

In 1935, a group called the Catfish Club was organized to run a slate against the C.C.A. candidates. From James Aston's Oral Report: "This group constituted the leadership of the community that was unhappy with the efficiency that had resulted from the reorganization of the city and the operation of it in the same manner that you would expect a corporation to operate." However, the Catfish Club convinced the majority of citizens and wiped out the C.C.A. slate for the next two elections.

When the Texas Centennial Exposition opened, it was Mayor George Sergeant, from the Catfish Club, who presided. The Centennial, which was the largest extravaganza Texas had ever seen, drew people from all over the country. President Franklin D. Roosevelt attended the Centennial. While he was in Dallas, he unveiled a statue of General Robert E. Lee in Oak Lawn Park, at which time the name was officially changed to Lee Park.

In 1937, Catfish Club candidate George Sprague became mayor. During his time in office, he fired City Manager Edy and put one of the Catfish Club members, Hal Mosely, in that position.

In 1939, the C.C.A. knew that they must regain control or it would be the end of their organization. It felt the Catfish Club had not been good for Dallas and had caused much dissension. C.C.A. President R.L. Thornton saved the association with his expert ability of uniting the group and campaigning. Two other groups had formed, one avowing to scrap the council-manager form of government. With three full slates of nine men and eight independents on the ballot, the entire C.C.A. slate won. Dallas Bar Association President Woodall Rodgers was elected mayor by the council and James Aston, who had been John Edy's assistant, was named the new city manager.

In 1941, the C.C.A. slate won again handily, and in 1943 and 1945, they were completely unopposed.

These were World War II years. Over fifty thousand Dallas men and women served in the armed forces, and at least that many more worked in war related jobs. The city of Dallas acquired Hensley Field, an airbase in Grand Prairie, and leased it to the government for military flights. It was used as a Navy Air Station. North American Aviation constructed a factory adjacent to Hensley

Field to build military aircraft. Other war related industries were in Garland, Irving, and other towns in Dallas County and the industries in the city of Dallas increased. This development began the urbanization of the county.

In 1947, forty-six men ran for council seats, with only Wallace Savage not having to go into a runoff to be elected. The council selected Jimmie Temple for mayor and Wallace Savage, mayor pro tem. During Temple's term, construction began on Central Expressway.

After World War II, Dallas was one of the first cities in the nation to enter the high tech industry. J. Erik Jonsson, Cecil Green, Pat Haggerty, and Eugene McDermott, all men with tremendous vision, decided to develop electronic manufacturing equipment. Their already successful company, Geophysical Service Incorporated, changed its name in 1951 to Texas Instruments. Through the next few years, Dallas attracted more high tech companies than any place in the country — companies such as Collins Radio, E-Systems, Rockwell to the latest, Fujitsu. Dallas was "high tech" before anyone else knew the term.

In 1949, Jean Baptist "Tiste" Adoue, Jr. won the largest number of votes when the C.C.A. slate was elected. Expecting to be selected mayor by the members of the council, Adoue was furious when they selected Wallace Savage instead.

Adoue, who had served as mayor pro tem in the last Woodall Rodgers administration, was head of one of the oldest banks in Dallas, The National Bank of Commerce. He had given service to the business and civic life of Dallas, having twice been president of the Chamber of Commerce. He also headed the Community Chest, and he had won the prestigious Linz Award for civic service in 1943. He seemingly had done everything to deserve to be the C.C.A. backed mayor. He, along with some of his friends, also C.C.A. members, demanded that the council call an election to pass a charter amendment providing for the mayor to be elected directly by the people. When the council refused, Adoue led the campaign himself to secure over 15,000 signatures on a petition to force an election. In his campaign, he denounced the power brokers of the C.C.A calling them "the palace guard of Dallas political kingdom." He told the citizens: "The powerful and influential downtown and Highland Park tycoons choose your mayor in secret meetings," according to Acheson in his book *Dallas Yesterday.* The people, in a special election in November 1949 approved the amendment, and it would take effect in 1951.

By this time, the C.C.A had forgiven Adoue and named him their candidate for mayor. He easily won.

Adoue's term as mayor was one of the most hectic two years in Dallas history. The council seldom agreed with him about anything. He tried to dismiss the city manager and the chief of police, moves which the council voted down. There was a water shortage. Heated disputes began regarding Love Field and a regional airport, but the administration resolved very little.

Before the 1953 election, the C.C.A sent S.J. Hay, a former president of the association, to appeal to Adoue not to run for reelection. Adoue formally removed himself from the race.

The election of R.L. (Bob) Thornton in 1953 began the most colorful, and possibly the most productive era in Dallas political history. These were the easy Eisenhower years of prosperity, and "Big D" certainly rode high upon the crest of those post-war years during all of Thornton's four terms as mayor.

The Trinity Industrial District was developed by John Stemmons in what was once the flood plain of the Trinity River. He and his friend, Trammell Crow, formed a partnership which created the world famous Dallas Market Center. Crow went on to become the nation's biggest land developer. Stemmons was one of the most influential behind the scenes politicians of the Citizens Charter Association and was one of Mayor Thornton's best friends. Mayor Thornton's favorite quote was "keep the dirt flyin'," and Dallas was certainly doing that. In addition to Stemmons' and Crow's industrial developments, Raymond Nasher and W.W. Overton developed commercial real estate. David G. Fox, owner of Fox and Jacobs built thousands of fashionable yet affordable homes in the Dallas area, while Mack Pogue's Lincoln Property Company was the leader of luxury apartments. The Henry Beck Company constructed skyscrapers throughout the city.

"Uncle Bob," as Thornton was known by many, was not a born and bred Dallasite. He was born in Hico County and had little schooling — a background which made his homespun manner of speaking even more attractive to urbane Dallasites. He was a frontiersman in the truest sense of the term, a tall and imposing figure, with a shock of white hair and alert eyes which looked straight at you from behind thick glasses. He rose to chairman of the board of the Mercantile National Bank, then one of the three largest banks in the city.

When the desegregation movement began, Mayor Thornton saw trouble ahead. He called the Citizens Council together, the organization of "yes" and "no" men which he had organized in 1935, instead of the City Council. He appealed to the membership for community-wide cooperation in integrating lunch counters, hotels, department stores, and other public facilities. He appointed C.A. Tatum, president of Dallas Power and Light Company and Sam Bloom, founder of Bloom Advertising Agency to spearhead a program of "smooth integration." Bloom produced a film titled, "Dallas at the Crossroads" which was shown to hundreds of church, school, and civic groups. They also enlisted the help of the media which cooperated one hundred percent. As a result of the carefully organized and meticulously planned campaign, Dallas suffered few of the racial uprisings experienced in other southern communities. One of the most serious of these conflicts took place in Marshall, Texas, where Bishop College students were in the forefront of anti-segregation demonstrations. Later, Dallas was to open its arms in welcome to the college which moved its entire campus to a site in the southern part of the city.

In 1959, the aging "Uncle Bob" had apparently decided to let up considerably in both his banking and city business and decided not to run for mayor again. There are varying versions of what happened at this point, but one version has it that Earle Cabell, a direct descendant of two mayors of Dallas history, was approached by the leaders of the Citizens Charter Association to run. He was ready and raring to go! Then suddenly, Thornton had a change of heart and called Earle Cabell to meet him at the City Club for lunch. "I've decided to go again after all," Uncle Bob announced. Cabell, shocked and more than a little miffed, replied, "Well, I'd hoped to run for the C.C.A, but I'm going to run anyway, as an independent."

Cabell, with the help of his well-known family and business, Cabell Dairies, gave Thornton a run for his money. In the process, he thoroughly irked the C.C.A which he claimed was trying to "hand-pick" and "dictate" who would be mayor. Thornton won the election, but only by a very small margin.

Two years later in 1961, at the age of 80, Thornton declared that four terms were enough. "I am not retiring, resigning or going around the world," he declared. "I have a great desire to remain a humble citizen of this great city of ours and to help in every cause that I can for the progress of our city." The era of Robert L. Thornton ended but it would never be forgotten. Probably his greatest contribution to the city he loved was his founding of the Citizens Council. The members of the Citizens Council, with their pride in and dedication to Dallas, have been the strength which has made Dallas thrive even through its most troubled years. The Citizens Council continues to be the guiding force today, 1991.

In the mayoralty campaign of 1961, television, then of the black and white variety, began to establish itself as a major influence on the electorate.

Earle Cabell had stepped on too many Citizens Council and Citizen Charter Associations members' toes in the 1959 campaign against the revered Bob Thornton to receive an endorsement just two years later. In fact, the C.C.A threw its considerable financial and political resource behind Joe Geary, a young attorney who was a part of the new Dallas establishment. But Cabell had just enough of the old-line Dallas name and establishment in himself that he would be sure to siphon off many C.C.A votes.

In the waning days of the campaign, Joe Geary was to face Earle Cabell in a major face-to-face debate before the Junior Chamber of Commerce at the Adolphus Hotel. Geary backers called the press, radio, and television news directors before the confrontation and told them to be prepared for a new development in the campaign.

Sure enough, Geary produced a police document which showed that Cabell had been arrested at the Red Barn Restaurant on Hillcrest Avenue for "disorderly conduct." Apparently Cabell had been arrested after an altercation in the restaurant parking lot.

The alert Cabell, when it came his turn to speak exclaimed dramatically, "Is there any man here who would not fight to protect the honor of his wife?" After the burst of applause subsided, many who were present at the debate frankly stated that they had changed their minds in favor of Earle Cabell. After it was reproduced by film on the nightly newscasts that evening, there were many observers who felt that the incident was the turning point in the campaign, and it proved to be true. Cabell narrowly defeated Geary 41,468 to 38,725. There were obviously many C.C.A votes in Cabell's total. The extraordinary power of television had definitely come into play in the outcome of the mayor's election in Dallas, Texas, as it had a year before in the presidential election of John F. Kennedy over Richard Nixon. Television in politics was apparently here to stay.

The 1960s found Dallas changing, as was most of the South. A new wave of ultraconservatives led by Congressman Bruce Alger became very vocal. Under the auspices of the Republican banner which lent them credibility, they staged pickets, insulted visiting statesmen, and accused anyone whose views differed from theirs of being a communist. The powerful leaders of the city were not a part of this group, but, seemed to close their eyes to the danger infiltrating the city. The atmosphere of this group brought such radicals as the John Birch Society which moved its headquarters to Dallas. A feeling of mistrust developed among the citizens of Dallas — a feeling that neither the city nor its people had ever known before.

Mayor Cabell seemed to enjoy calling himself an "independent" after his victory without C.C.A support. In 1963, he proposed something previously unheard of in Dallas. According to his plan, 3,000 public housing units, paid for by the federal government, would be built — half for the aged and half for low-income Blacks. But the Dallas Real Estate Board, made up of many of the most influential developers and builders, fought it.

As historian A.C. Greene observes in his contribution to the Dallas Mayors Oral History Project, "...Dallas was very proud that it would not accept federal funding, no federal financing, for any of its programs. And Dallas as a city, suffered a great deal for this attitude. But it is an attitude which has permeated Dallas political and governmental history forever."

Cabell appealed to the Citizens Council to no avail. Finally, the matter was brought to the voters and the mayor's proposal was overwhelmingly defeated.

But this was certainly not Cabell's greatest disaster. On November 22, 1963, riding in the presidential motorcade of John F. Kennedy, Cabell, with his wife "Dearie" at his side, heard a volley of gunshots echo among the concrete and brick of the County Courthouse, the triple underpass, and a building which would go down in history, the Texas School Book Depository Building.

The assassination of President Kennedy would change the future of the nation and the world. In Dallas, it would change the makeup of government and politics for years to come. People from all over the world blamed Dallas for this tragic event. Dallas became known as the "city of hate" because of the small group of radicals who had distributed "Wanted for Treason" pamphlets showing President Kennedy's picture the day before he arrived. Hours before the assassination, a full-page ad appeared in *The Dallas Morning News* challenging the President to defend himself against the charges. The fact however, was that thousands of Dallas' citizens lined the streets to cheer the President and the First Lady. No place in the world was more devastated than the city of Dallas, Texas.

On February 3, 1964, Cabell resigned the office of mayor to run for the United States Congress against the incumbent Bruce Alger. The moderate Democrat was backed by the "establishment" and became one of Dallas' most successful congressmen.

After Mayor Cabell's resignation, one of the most unusual events in Dallas political history occurred. Following are several versions reported in the Dallas Public Library Mayor Oral History Reports:

A.C. Greene: "We picked up *The Dallas Morning News* — and I say this as the (then) editor of the editorial page of *The Times Herald* — and discovered that Erik Jonsson had been named our new mayor. Quite a few of the city council members didn't know it either, and there was a great deal of, 'Hey, why didn't somebody tell me?' This was sort of hushed up rather quickly, and nobody really complained. It wasn't that anybody had anything against Erik Jonsson. He was well-respected, and I think Erik Jonsson is a very intelligent, a very human person. But it was a bit of a shock to have a city of, at that time, six hundred or so thousand wake up and read the morning newpaper and discover who their mayor was."

John Stemmons: "...So the Citizens Charter Association, which was then the primary group that would elect councilmen and that sort of thing and make sure that we had good people went to Erik Jonsson — I was one of them that went with them — and asked him if he wouldn't take over the mayor's job. Now we went because we had talked with members of the city council who had that right kind of appointment and they wanted someone of that character. And that's how Erik Jonsson got to be mayor originally — he was appointed by the city council."

Councilwoman (during that time) Elizabeth Blessing: "We did not know one thing. Not one thing. We did not know about the meeting. I had rumors of it the day of the council meeting, and I don't know exactly whether that came...I can't remember whether that came from someone in the press...But (fellow councilman) George Underwood, himself told me...He sat by me all those years and he wouldn't mind me divulging this because this is what happened. He said, 'They are going to bring in a really big name to be on the council (and) make him mayor.'"

The late Larry Kelly, then the executive director of the Dallas Civic Opera, was quoted in Leslie Warren's *Dallas Public and Private:* "I think we have the only city in the world where it could happen. Any other place there'd be a thousand pickets down there protesting it. *Somebody* for *some* reason, has to be against him. But not a peep in Dallas."

The Citizens Council's men felt that Dallas needed a special kind of person to bring the city out of the negative national and even international image that the President's assassination had left upon the community.

J. Erik Jonsson who had come to Dallas from Brooklyn, New York, was one of the men who had established Texas Instruments. He certainly met the C.C.A criteria for "coming up through the chairs," having just served as president of the Citizens Council as well as the Chamber of Commerce. He had been active in all civic organizations and was president of a hugely successful business. He was the kind of person needed at this sensitive time. The city council appointed him mayor.

Mayor Jonsson, with his dynamic spirit and vision, began a program called "Goals for Dallas." This program was set by a committee of citizens and served as a great rebuttal to the argument that the well-heeled in Dallas had no regard for anything but progress and money. It proved them to have a heart.

The city continued to prosper, the skyscrapers continued to soar into the sky, and Jonsson coasted back into office in 1965, 1967, and 1969.

The computer age had begun, and Dallas, always at the forefront of new ventures, was the Texas headquarters for International Business Machines (IBM). An IBM salesman in the early sixties, Ross Perot is quoted by Arthur Lewis in *Fortune Magazine* as saying, "We were getting the hardware into place, but the customers weren't getting what they wanted. They would hire a staff and then proceed by trial and error. It was comparable to getting steel and concrete for a building before buying a lot." Perot had a vision to develop systems designed to fit the individual needs of the customer. On July 27, 1962, on his 32nd birthday, he incorporated Electronic Data Systems (EDS). The firm provided data processing systems to a small number of large-size companies. It had four divisions: financial institutions, life insurance companies, health insurance companies, and retailing. This radically new concept in data processing began with one man and one thousand dollars, and in less than six years, it became a three hundred million dollar company. In 1968, Fortune Magazine said, "Probably no man has ever made so much money so fast." In the early 1980s Perot sold EDS to General Motors Corporation for 2.5 billion dollars. True to the Dallas spirit, his philanthropic accomplishments are seen throughout the city, state, country, and world.

Pro football arrived in Dallas in 1960, when Clint Murchison, Jr. bought the Dallas franchise in the National Football League and named his team the Dallas Cowboys. Tom Landry, a former star at the University of Texas, was the first coach and continued to be head coach until 1989. Tex Schramm, a genius in football management, ran the club for Murchison. The Cowboys struggled the first few years; picked up in the late '60s; and finally got to the Super Bowl in 1972, but lost to the Baltimore Colts. But in 1973, as a result of Schramm's shrewd scouting system, Murchison's money, Landry's famous flex defense, and players like Roger Staubach, Bob Lilly, and Lee Roy Jordan, the Dallas Cowboys became World Champions in Super Bowl VIII by defeating the Miami Dolphins. From then on, the Dallas Cowboys were known as "America's Team."

While Perot was building his empire, and the Dallas Cowboys were making a name for themselves, Mayor Jonsson's greatest achievement was the success of the Crossroads Bond Program, which included the Dallas/Fort Worth Regional Airport. This was the most ambitious single bond program in the history of the city. During the bond campaign, the city of Jefferson, Texas, was cited as a campaign example with the famous phrase "grass would grow in the streets of Jefferson" if they did not encourage the railroads to come through their town. Of course, Dallas got the railroads and Jefferson did not. During the course of the campaign, an ambitious reporter named Jim Underwood called the current mayor of Jefferson by telephone and told him of the campaign technique being used by the supporters of the Crossroads bond issue. When the reporter asked if grass was growing in the streets, to his surprise, the mayor said, "That's right son!" All counts in the bond program passed easily.

When Jonsson proposed the striking I.M. Pei-designed city hall, many citizens balked at the somewhat drastic cantilever design. In fact, near the end of his term, the entire issue of the new city hall had become so controversial that Jonsson called a news conference to withdraw the plans entirely, and for a time it appeared that this would be Mayor Jonsson's greatest political and governmental disappointment.

In 1970, near the end of his last term in office, *Look* magazine awarded Dallas the coveted "All America City" award. Dallas had finally overcome the blame for the tragic events of November 22, 1963.

There were brief hints in 1970 that Jonsson might run again, but Jonsson was tired, his wife was ill, and he stood by his decision to retire.

Describing what the C.C.A looks for in selecting their candidates, former C.C.A president John Stemmons says in his Mayors Oral History Report, "you take all of the people that have reached particular promise in your business community and in the professional community, have gone through the chairs, they've been expected to run cards for the United Way, they've been expected to run cards and solicit for the hospitals or the churches or the various sundry things that go on in Dallas. They are expected to devote a certain amount of time to help put over a bond issue or fight somebody that's evil."

Strangely enough, after a long and successful history of bringing prospective mayoral candidates "up through the chairs" of civic service, the Citizens Charter Association found itself searching for a strong candidate to challenge a popular former sportscaster-turned-councilman, Wes Wise, in 1971.

Wes Wise was practically a household name. Beginning in 1949, he had broadcast play by play the baseball

"Game of the Day" with "the Old Scotchman," Gordon McLendon, on L.B.S., the Liberty Broadcasting System, headquartered in Dallas. Later, he was the sports anchor for Dallas' major televison stations, first for channel 8 and then for channel 4. Dallas had always been an enthusiastic sports town and the friendly sportscaster was well known and well liked all over the city. In addition, as a councilman, Wise had not hesitated to oppose the C.C.A majority, and came to be known as something of a maverick.

The C.C.A finally chose a tall, personable construction contractor from Oak Cliff named Avery Mays to oppose Wise. But Mays, an inexperienced speaker, was no match for Wise, whose entire career had been professional radio-television. When Mays at first refused to appear for a debate, Wise would bring out an "empty chair" emphasizing his opponent's absence.

Wise maintained he only needed to get into the runoff to win, and he made it, though behind Mays by 5,000 votes. In the runoff, although outspent nearly 5-to-1 by the C.C.A, *The Dallas Times Herald* headlined, "Wise Wins in a Walk," as he tallied 57,776 votes to Mays' 39,947.

Wise came into the office during the worst of the Vietnam protest era. While it was not a local issue, the protestors still haunted the nation's council chambers and Dallas was no exception.

Racial slurs at the council became commonplace. Black civic leaders warned the Dallas City Council that "blood will flow in the streets" if it did not change its ways, especially concerning newly-imposed school busing to achieve racial balance in the schools. Wise worked diligently with Black leaders to keep peace in the schools.

Wise, with a strong minority vote, seemed to calm

these fears. Known already as "the people's mayor," he started his "open door policy," setting aside several hours once a week "to meet and talk with anyone who wants to come see the mayor." More blacks attended these weekly Wednesday afternoon meetings than any other identifiable group.

George Schrader, originally brought to the city by Jonsson, became city manager with Wise's support. He said of Wise in his Mayor's Oral Report: "...Mayor Wise was one who came in and who gave that relief — sense of relief — and responded to the need of an association with many who missed that association with Mayor Jonsson or who never had association with previous mayors. A great deal was accomplished..."

Dallas won the coveted AAA bond rating and Mayor Wise personally led the campaigns of two successful bond elections which "kept the dirt flyin'" in the Dallas tradition.

Wise's first term was marked with surprisingly little dissension, although every member of his council either was or had been a C.C.A. candidate.

Alex Bickley who served as city attorney for both Mayor Jonsson and Mayor Wise, but who has always been closely identified with the side of the Dallas establishment, is quoted in his oral history report as saying: "...Well, I think Wise's administration was different from the others because he came in as the independent out there who was fighting the so-called establishment. And so this required him to do some things that he might not have done otherwise because he had to maintain that image...and it was a consistent image and I think a fair one. I would say this, that it made it harder for him to get programs across that he would liked to have seen because the majority of the council was still the other group, and so he many times was having to fight for the things that he wanted there in the council without a majority. But I'll say this, that with Mayor Wise, I found him to be very fair..."

Wise's style changed somewhat from independent to a mayor "hell-bent" on conciliation and compromise, which did not always please his best backers. "When you're mayor," he said, "you have to be mayor for all the people, not just those who have always agreed with you," he told me in an interview in 1984. Actually, Wise did not consider himself "anti-establishment" as some people thought.

The early 1970s brought much prosperity to Dallas. Businesses clamored to move their headquarters to Dallas. People from less prosperous areas of the country swarmed to Dallas. The most popular show on television was named "Dallas" and the Dallas Cowboys football team was called "America's Team." Dallas was riding high. The city continued to prosper even in the midst of one of the nation's worst recessions.

The Dallas-Fort Worth Airport was opened with much fanfare as relations between the two cities reached an all-time high. Mayor Wise of Dallas and Mayor Stovall of Ft. Worth became fast friends and toured the country and the world together to secure international air carriers for DFW Airport, and they succeeded.

Wise was able to convince the city council to revive the new city hall project. As City Manager Schrader observes in his oral report, "Mayor Wise endorsed the project and succeeded in resolving it. Whether Mayor Jonsson would have ever been able to achieve that is unknown. But certainly Mayor Wise was able to do that to his great credit...he provided the personal presence and style that got this building under contract and passed those bond issues (in 1972 and 1975)." Former Mayor Jonsson, at the City Hall opening, said "It was Wes who got the contract signed."

In 1973, the Citizens Charter Association sent several of its members to Wise regarding a possible endorsement but he declined, declaring: "This would be a betrayal to those who have voted for me because of my independence." He won over a field of five other candidates, with the highest percentage of the vote of any contested election in Dallas history to that time.

Mayor Wise was instrumental in obtaining many important conventions, including the biggest of all, the National Association of Home Builders. During his second term, *Newsweek* magazine cited Dallas as "the city that works."

In 1975, the C.C.A decided to field the young and vigorous president of the association, John Schoellkopf, who was a member of an old and very prominent family. The popular mayor, however, won again overwhelmingly.

That defeat spelled the end of the C.C.A. This was the last election in which the C.C.A was to run a candidate under their banner.

On January 17, 1975, U.S. District Judge Eldon Mahon ruled the at-large method of electing all council members illegally discriminated against minorities. The old-guard business oligarchs felt that single member districts would ruin the council-manager form of government which had kept city hall free of corruption since it was installed in 1931 and would lead to "ward politics." City Attorney Alex Bickley offered the court an 8-3 mixed system, meaning that eight of the council members would be elected in single member districts, while three members including the mayor would be elected citywide. The argument was that some citywide representation was a good balancer. Over the vehement objections of the minority plainiffs, who wanted all eleven members elected in districts and the mayor to be selected by the council, Judge Mahon finally agreed to the 8-3 plan in 1979. Preserving three at-large positions was a brilliant move by City Attorney Bickley. The single member district plan took over four years to resolve.

In the spring of 1976, Mayor Wise resigned as mayor to run for United States Congress. In a special election a heated race for mayor by two former C.C.A leaders, Garry Weber and Bob Folsom, emerged. Neither wanted to run under the banner of the C.C.A as they both felt it would be the kiss of death.

Both men were multi-millionaires. Garry Weber, a current city councilman, owned a highly successful stock brokerage company. Bob Folsom was one of the most successful developers in Dallas. Both had been popular football players for Southern Methodist University; Weber during the Don Meredith era and Folsom with the great Doak Walker. Both had been involved in many business and civic interests. They were both examples of the C.C.A candidate of the past.

The C.C.A had met earlier with R.L. Thornton, Jr., son of the former mayor, suggesting to him that he be their candidate. Folsom, hearing of this meeting, called the top leaders of the C.C.A informing them that he had decided to run, but not if they were fielding a candidate, according to Mayor Folsom's oral report. They immediately withdrew their offer to Thornton.

Weber, already on the council, had been considered an able candidate to move into the mayor's chair prior to Folsom entering the race. However, Folsom beat Weber with less than 1,000 votes difference.

Folsom won easily with practically no opposition in the 1977 regular city election. Because of the delay of the courts in approving the single member district plan, this council was compelled to remain in office until the decision was reached near the end of 1979. The next election was not until January 1980.

During Folsom's administration, the 18,000 seat Reunion Arena was completed, and Folsom pushed hard for a National Basketball Association (NBA) team to come to Dallas. Dallas businessman Donald Carter also wanted to have basketball become part of Dallas, and when the NBA voted to have two expansion teams for the 1980-81 season, Carter immediately put together a group of businessmen to apply for a franchise. With expert athletic fundraiser Norm Sonju, Carter and his investors got the franchise, and the Dallas Mavericks team was born.

During his tenure, Folsom was constantly under fire by many newly established homeowners' organizations. He continued the north Dallas advancement by annexing the town of Renner opening up the north for future annexation.

Building was running rampant, not only in far north Dallas, but in the suburbs, especially in Plano, Farmers Branch, Richardson, Carrollton and Addison.

A new city had been perfectly designed near Irving, called Las Colinas, most of which had been the Carpenter ranch. This perfectly planned city, between Dallas and D/FW Airport, attracted many businesses from across the country to move their headquarters there, rather than into the city limits of Dallas.

The education system was beginning to feel the results of the forced busing ordered in 1975 by Judge William Taylor. Affluent families placed children in private schools.

Many white upper class families moved to the suburbs, which were growing by leaps and bounds. The Dallas Independent School District system suffered during this period.

With the expansion of the convention center and the completion of Reunion Arena, Dallas was attracting some of the largest conventions and biggest entertainers in the country. The Reunion Tower Ball with its thousands of lights, kept time to the music of the radio station inside the tower.

Folsom decided not to run for another term. He called his friend, Jack Evans, saying. "Jack, ...all the folks I talk to say that Jack Evans should run for mayor." (Mayor Jack Evans' oral report). The control of the "new wave" establishment was continued and probably even strengthened. Jack Evans was elected mayor in 1981.

Evans was a protege of the C.C.A leaders Bob and Charles Cullum. He was an executive of the Cullum Company, a large grocery store chain. The Cullums had always been influential in the Citizens Charter Association, the Citizens Council, and the State Fair of Texas. Evans met all the requirements of what had been the Citizens Charter Association criteria. He had headed numerous civic drives and he was well-known and well-respected in the business community.

Quoting from Mayor Evans Oral History Library Project, Evans said about the C.C.A, "I think it had the leadership of about six or eight people. I think, for the most part, the others were people who wanted to associate with those six or eight people because of the power. The power was there. I personally didn't like that. I think when you vest too much power in any group, it is dangerous. But I thank and appreciate a lot of people that were there. I don't think they knowingly exerted their power to the degree that they did at the expense of the city and the citizens of the community...We've been very fortunate, I think, in Dallas leadership."

Though Evans was a very good friend of the immediate past mayor, Robert Folsom, unlike Folsom, he was a very personable man. Again quoting Evans from the Oral History, "Bob was not a person-sensitive person. He is a hard-nosed, tough-minded businessperson and deals with the bottom line and did not give people a lot of time. Some councilpeople who had been in office since I've been there said it was the first time they had entered the mayor's office. They didn't feel comfortable dealing with him because of his style. To me, that doesn't take anything away from Bob Folsom. That just happened to be his style, and it was effective. He is a successful person. Mine is different. I want people to come in. I want to talk with them."

In a special section on Dallas progress, *The Dallas Morning News* headlined on October 16, 1983, "The Dallas area led the nation in office building construction in the last twelve months." In downtown, four major high-rise projects were going up: the seventy-story Interfirst Plaza at Elm and Griffin, which would be Dallas' tallest skyscraper, the fifty-story LTV Center adjacent to the arts district, the forty-five-story Lincoln Plaza at the triangle of Akard, Ervay and Ross and the three building complex of Southwestern Bell Telephone at Commerce and Akard. The old Higginbotham-Bailey Building, a long time Dallas landmark, was renovated to become the Founders Building.

Mayor Evans had to deal with a most indecisive council. The traffic problem on Central Expressway had become intolerable, so much so that the State Highway Department agreed to pay to double-deck it or expand it, since it was also Highway 75. At first the council voted "yes," then when the homeowner groups complained, they reversed their decision. This issue bounced about such a long time that the State finally said they would use their money elsewhere. Evans felt that the city needed to get some of the money the city sent to Washington returned to Dallas for various projects. The old conservative idea that Dallas would have no part of federal assistance still existed and the council couldn't decide what to do. Quoting Evans from his Oral Report, "We have found ourselves, in Dallas, that we've lived in clandestine situations. That is, if you live in Highland Park and everything is nice, you have no problems with worrying about paying the grocery bill or utility bill, or whatever. Then if you live in south Dallas, the poverty levels there, the housing projects...without federal funding, what can we do to this thing? In a city that is thriving with a robust economy, how can we correct that without federal funding?" He finally convinced the council of the need for a representative in Washington. In a lengthy process that took eight months, the council members selected a representative, only to change their minds and table the whole issue two weeks later. These were only two of the many issues this city council could not resolve.

Evans, practically acting alone, got the newly approved Arts District going by working with the private sector of the community. He secured the Republican National Convention to be in Dallas in 1984. Probably his biggest accomplishment was the successful bond election which raised a one percent sales tax for the much needed, long sought-after mass transit system, Dallas Area Rapid Transit (DART).

Heavy pressures were obviously on Evans. He chose not to seek reelection in 1983. Bob Folsom's former campaign manager, Starke Taylor, decided to take his turn.

Homeowner groups, minorities, and citizens who felt that the development in north Dallas had reached near-critical stages, urged former mayor Wes Wise to challenge Taylor.

Folsom said, in his oral history report, that he knew no one any more competitive than himself with the exception of Starke Taylor. Taylor said he would run only if he were certain that he would win. Certainty meant one thing — money. Taylor, with the aid of a highly paid campaign consultant and highly paid media advisors, was able to saturate the local television market with his own name and image. At the same time, a considerable negative campaign was directed at Wise. With the thousands of newcomers to the city, this television coverage paid off. While the former mayor tallied nearly 48% of the votes on less than $65,000, Starke Taylor, spending just under $1,000,000, became mayor in 1983.

Taylor appointed citizen task forces to tackle problems from lead contamination and traffic congestion, to crime and economic development. As Taylor explained, "I figured the more people we had involved in City Hall, the better off we'd be. A mayor and city council can't do it all." Although his critics said he had too many people with too many different opinions, these citizen task forces were one of his most memorable achievements.

Early in his administration, the council voted to increase the limit of political contributions for mayoral elections to $5,000 per person. Taylor staged a dinner which raised $800,000 repaying his personal loan to his previous campaign and assuring his reelection.

Douglas Lyons, in *The Dallas Times Herald* on November 21, 1986, reported that Taylor opposed city funding for several programs to aid the homeless saying "I think the private sector has to solve these problems."

George Rodrigue wrote in *The Dallas Morning News* on April 27, 1987: "Trying to encourage more private sector participation, Taylor shocked the elite Salesmanship Club of Dallas in a speech, painting a graphic picture of the deplorable living conditions in public housing units in West Dallas, urging their help. 'I doubt if any of you have ever been over there,' he said."

During the summer of 1984, Dallas hosted the Republican National Convention. Exhibiting the same spirit that Dallas citizens have shown since the days of John Neely Bryan, Democrats and Independents worked side by side with Republicans to show the nation what Dallas was all about. The renomination of one of the all-time most popular presidents, Ronald Reagan, seemed almost secondary as Dallas, through the efforts of all citizens, pooled their money, time and energy to entertain the visitors. Television cameras confirmed the already universal image that Dallas was the place to be!

Taylor spearheaded the council's appointment of Dallas' first black city manager, Richard Knight, when City Manager Charles Anderson resigned to head the Dallas Area Rapid Transit Authority.

The mayor became known for his hot temper at city council meetings. Homeowners' President Larry Duncan described Mayor Taylor as being anti-neighborhood. Duncan was quoted by Henry Tatum in *The Dallas Morning News* on March 4, 1984, as saying, "His record as mayor on issues were far and away in favor of the developers interests whenever they differed from neighborhood interests."

In 1985, Max Goldblatt, an outspoken city councilman, was Taylor's only semi-serious opposition. He ran his entire campaign against DART (Dallas Area Rapid Transit). and its plan for future transportation. He favored a monorail to the light rail and bus proposal of DART. He made a fairly good showing against Taylor, however, Taylor was elected for a second term.

In the mid-1980s, the drop in oil prices sent shock waves through Texas banks. The Dallas economy held out longer than many Texas cities. However, oil debts coupled with bad real estate loans sent leading institutions spiraling. Massive real estate development and overbuilding had gone unchecked. It was said that in far north Dallas, at the height of the building boom, one real estate deal could change hands three times in twenty-four hours involving millions and millions of dollars. Hundreds of developers became millionaires overnight. Then Dallas real estate crashed. Thousands of commercial and residential properties went into foreclosure. Office buildings were left empty. Landlords offered free rent for up to three years in order to attract tennants. Some of the largest lending institutions in Dallas went belly-up and were taken over by the federal government. Once-prominent businessmen were now faced with criminal suits, bankers found themselves unemployed, and the entire construction industry came to a screeching halt. Record bankruptcies and business failures caused city-wide unemployment. In addition, the city budget was facing a deficit.

Dallas had always housed big businesses and relied on their tax money. For years, companies had been moving out of downtown and to the suburbs. It was said businesses were flocking to Dallas, but in reality they were relocating in the Dallas area — outside the city limits. While Dallas serviced all of the area in many ways, the revenue to the city was declining in proportion. The inner city was attracting the poor, the mentally ill street people, the homeless, and crime increased to a frightening degree.

Shopping centers had gone up all over the city and in the suburbs, and downtown shopping had become almost non-existent. By the end of the '80s all of the major department stores except Neiman-Marcus had moved out of downtown Dallas.

After having experienced a great deal of physical pain, the mayor had surgery and decided he would not seek a third term.

Starke Taylor wept at his November 1986 news conference in which he announced his retirement. "I don't want to duck out on Dallas during a critical time," he added, "but the Lord is the only one really watching over Dallas. I've just been privileged to help Him a little in His job."

Taylor said that getting the final approval for the expansion of North Central Expressway was one of the highlights of his tenure.

Listing some of his setbacks, the mayor cited the failure to get more investments in southern Dallas and to coordinate health services in Dallas County. He also said race relations needed to be improved.

Dallas had many problems in 1987. The city led the nation in crime and the economy was the lowest in history.

As soon as Mayor Taylor announced that he would not seek a third term, Mayor Pro Tem Annette Strauss declared herself a candidate.

A very dynamic woman, Mrs. Strauss was the wife of multi-millionaire Theodore Strauss and sister-in-law of former Democratic National Chairman Robert Strauss. Annette Strauss, however, was a Dallas legend in her own right. She had worked diligently for every legitimate cause in the city for over 40 years. She had raised millions of dollars for the arts, she had chaired every major charity drive in the city and won nearly every community service award. She was a devoted wife and mother, and in recent years she had served on numerous city boards and had completed two terms on the city council.

Realizing the extreme conflict in the city, true to the Dallas spirit, some other prominent citizens came forward to run for mayor. These men, like Mrs. Strauss, truly wanted to give their expertise and abilities to help solve the problems. Two of the most prominent were Jim Collins and Fred Meyer.

Former Congressman Jim Collins had served his constituents well in Washington. He and his family had been leaders in the community and had given generously of their wealth to many causes. Fred Meyer, former Republican County chairman, was a very successful businessman and a leader in the community.

Strauss was especially solicitous of Blacks and Hispanics. They turned out in unusually high numbers and gave her 90% of their votes. They proudly wore t-shirts boasting "ANNIE'S ARMY." "Women for Strauss" also rallied to help make Dallas history. She spent 1.2 million dollars to capture the job with fund raisers from $5.00 to $500.00.

Although Annette Strauss won 48% of the vote, she was placed in a runoff with Fred Meyer and won handily with 57% of the votes.

History was made in Dallas on April 18, 1987, when it elected it's first woman mayor. Annette Strauss declared to her supporters and to a national television audience, "Dallas is ready for a woman mayor — and for those few who are not, here I come anyway!"

The issues she faced were numerous and of great magnitude. Crime had risen, police and minority relationships were not good. The quality and stability of neighborhoods were at risk. Economic development, especially in southern Dallas, was a continuing problem. Environment, drugs, human services, and health problems were major priorities.

Dallas' first woman mayor certainly had her hands full! Mayor Strauss's style was markedly different from Taylor's. Fresh flowers often decorated her desk and she kept a brightly decorated candy jar labeled "Annette's Constituent Candy." She was a moderate and she was eager to please. Her willingness to listen caused her critics to call her indecisive and question her ability to lead, but supporters praised her tolerance.

As the first elected female mayor of Dallas, she drastically increased the number of women appointed to city boards and commissions. She said, "Women should not be afraid to try anything, and whatever their goal may be, they should go for it."

In addition to the many problems facing the city, her council was most difficult. Some of them were interested in their own agendas and some delighted in media attention.

Mayor Strauss, in her reelection in 1989, had the last five mayors of Dallas supporting her — Starke Taylor, Jack Evans, Bob Folsom, Wes Wise, and Erik Jonsson.

Several incidents were pressing. A petition was filed by firefighters to require the council to add 130 more to their force. The Dallas Police Association wanted to get rid of the Citizens Review Board. Minorities were still having problems with the police. DART, the transit system, had spent millions of dollars and little had been accomplished.

"We are going through a lot of changes and they are going to be painful, but they are going to happen," Strauss said in early 1989. "I'm sure it was my fault that the Dallas Cowboys had such a lousy season," she joked. The opening of the I.M. Pei-designed building called The Morton H. Myerson Symphony Hall, and nicknamed "The Mort," was the highlight for the citizens of Dallas in 1989. The Meyerson, the latest addition to the Dallas Arts District, was considered the most magnificent symphony hall in the country.

Mayor Strauss was an outstanding goodwill ambassador for Dallas. She made several trips to Washington D.C., lobbying for money for various projects. She travelled to numerous cities and countries encouraging businesses to come to Dallas. She was instrumental in bringing such corporations as J.C. Penney and Fujitsu to the metroplex.

When City Manager Richard Knight resigned to go into private business, the council appointed Jan Hart the first woman city manager.

The 1990 census was announced showing Dallas to be only forty-eight percent white. The minorities were now the majority in the city.

Severe city charter problems had begun in 1989 when Roy Williams and Marvin Crenshaw, two unsuccessful at-large candidates, filed a lawsuit alleging the current municipal government system discriminated against African-Americans. The Ledbetter Neighborhood Association, which represented a group of hispanic residents in west Dallas, joined the litigaton as interveners. U.S. District Judge Jerry Buchmeyer issued a ruling to order a special election to choose all council members from single member districts.

The council designed a plan to give minorities more

seats called the 10-4-1 plan. This plan called for ten single member districts, four at-large area districts, and the mayor elected at-large throughout the city. An election was held, and 10-4-1 was approved by the people.

Judge Buchmeyer, however, with opposition from the plantiffs, rejected the plan, and demanded a 14-1 system. The council went back to the drawing boards and designed a 14-1 plan. Many council members opposed the plan, and when it went before the people, it was narrowly defeated. When Judge Buchmeyer ordered a council election under 14-1 anyway, the council took the issue to the higher court in New Orleans. This court agreed to allow Dallas to take the matter to the Justice Department in Washington, D.C.

Meanwhile, the present city council members' terms had expired but they were compelled to stay until this matter was resolved. Mayor Strauss however, announced that she would not seek a third term.

After the Justice Department rejected the 10-4-1 plan in May of 1991, Mayor Strauss persuaded the majority of the council to agree to the 14-1 plan. The fourteen single-member districts with the mayor elected at-large plan was designed. Judge Buchmeyer ordered a city election to be held in November 1991. During this long dispute, racial tensions surfaced as never before between Whites, Hispanics, and Blacks. Mayor Strauss, with her ability to communicate with all ethnic groups, kept the tense situation from getting to a riotous stage.

Former Mayor Jack Evans said of Dallas' first woman mayor: "I think Annette Strauss was the best mayor we could have had the past few years. She was the right mayor at the right time."

Since his term as mayor, Evans had become the leader of the power group in Dallas. He was named chairman of the Citizens Council and that group and other business people turned to him for guidance.

For nearly five years, Dallas had continued in economic turmoil. The need for city services grew with the recession, yet tax increases were not welcomed by the near bankrupt companies and homeowners with less money. The city found itself in the paradox of increased needs and falling means. The city had to tighten its budget by cutting so-called non-essential services. The first council with the 14-1 configuration, to be elected in November 1991, had many difficult decisions facing them.

Our current leaders are already working toward the twenty-first century. Mayor Strauss has been to Mexico and plans a trip to Canada soon. She wants to see Dallas become the "Economic Capital" of North America. She would like to see D/FW airport be the hub for the three nations when Congress lifts the trade restrictions. Former Mayor Jack Evans was a leader in the successful campaign for Congress to give Dallas, in conjunction with Ellis County, the Superconducting Super Collider, the scientific phenomenon of the future.

Challenging times — exciting times — lay ahead for the city of Dallas. Each of us is being called to vote, to participate, to make a commitment in assuring a glorious future.

Mayor Thornton's statement, made in 1955, is even more significant today: "I would like to see the old indomitable Dallas spirit revived and embraced by our citizens... it is the spirit of the people of a city that *makes* and *keeps* a city great."

EPILOGUE

In November 1991, we will celebrate "Jubilee Dallas," commemorating our 150th birthday.

As we prepare for this celebration, we should look back to the past accomplishments and our proud heritage. We should remember the men and women whose spirit and vision gave us the first Texas railroads, made Dallas the cotton capital of the world, and a leader in banking and insurance. We should look with pride to the recent leaders and their development of the Dallas/Fort Worth International Airport, the Dallas Convention Center, the Dallas Market Center, the University of Texas Southwestern Medical Center and the new state-of-the-art Morton H. Myerson Symphony Hall and Arts District.

The special character that Dallas has maintained through the years comes from men and women from every social, economic, political, religious, and racial strata who have taken a personal interest in building a great city. Dallas has been fortunate and unique to have had so many families interested in the fortunes and future of their city, who have given their time, money, and efforts to ensure its success.

John Neely Bryan's log cabin has a special place in downtown Dallas. The memorable home of the first man of "Dallas Spirit" is illuminated by the big ball of Reunion Tower, which signifies the men and women who followed him with that same great spirit.

And the legacy of "Dallas Spirit" lives on...

John Neely Bryan and wife, Margaret
Courtesy Dallas Public Library

John Neely Bryan Cabin
Courtesy Dallas Public Library

Iron Bridge (1860) connecting Dallas to Oak Cliff
Courtesy Dallas Public Library

Houston Street viaduct today
Courtesy John Douglas Cheney

Sanger Brothers Dry Goods Store (1872) — Alex Sanger
Courtesy Dallas Public Library

First Dallas Professional Baseball Team (1888)
Courtesy Dallas Public Library

Horse-drawn Streetcar on Ervay Street (1873)
Courtesy Dallas Public Library

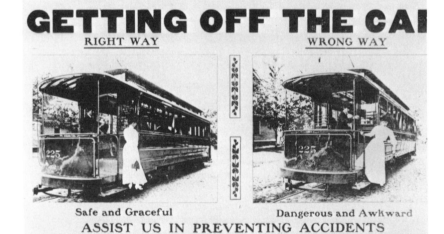

Electric Streetcar (1890)
Courtesy Dallas Public Library

First Railroad Station (1885)
Courtesy Dallas Public Library

Union Station
Courtesy Dallas Public Library

George Bannerman Dealey
Courtesy Dallas Public Library

Mayor Frank W. Wozencraft (1919–1921) and son
Courtesy Dallas Public Library

"Old Red" Courthouse in center of city square (1891)
Courtesy Dallas Public Library

"Old Red" Courthouse today (1991)
Courtesy John Douglas Cheney

Akard Street looking south (about 1930)
Courtesy Dallas Public Library

The Ku Klux Klan 1923 — an effort to break the Dallas Spirit

Triple underpass under construction (1935)
Courtesy Dallas Public Library

Triple underpass completed
Courtesy Dallas Public Library

St. Paul Sanitarium (1898)

Parkland Hospital (1894)

Baylor Sanitarium (1910)
Photos courtesy Dallas Public Library

Baker Hotel Ballroom (1926)
Courtesy Dallas Public Library

Oriental Hotel (1893)
Courtesy Dallas Public Library

Adolphus Hotel (1910)
Courtesy Dallas Public Library

Texas State Fair (1903)
Courtesy Dallas Public Library

State Fair of Texas (1908)
Courtesy Dallas Public Library

*President Franklin D. Roosevelt
speaks at Texas Centennial (1936)*
Courtesy Dallas Public Library

Crowd in Cotton Bowl hears President Roosevelt (1936)
Courtesy Dallas Public Library

Mayor Charles Turner
(1932–1935)

Mayor George Sergeant *Mayor George A. Sprague*
(1935–1937) *(1937–1939)*

Photos courtesy Dallas Public Library

Dedication of Robert E. Lee statue in Lee Park (1936)
Courtesy Dallas Public Library

Love Field Airport
Courtesy Aviation Department, City of Dallas

Dallas Club Building (1900)
Courtesy Dallas Public Library

"Flying Red Horse"
atop Magnolia Building
Courtesy Dallas Public Library

Neiman–Marcus
Courtesy Dallas Public Library

Cumberland Hill Elementary School (1905)
now Sedco, Akard St. & Woodall Rogers Freeway
Courtesy Dallas Public Library

Southern Methodist University (1915) now Dallas Hall of S.M.U.
Courtesy Dallas Public Library

City Hall (1888)
Courtesy Dallas Public Library

City Hall (1912)
Courtesy Dallas Public Library

Mayor Woodall Rodgers (1939–1947)
Courtesy Dallas Public Library

Mayor J.R. Temple (1947–1949) center
Courtesy Dallas Public Library

Mayor Wallace Savage (1949–1951)
Courtesy Dallas Public Library

Mayor J.B. Adoue, Jr. (1951–1953)
Courtesy Dallas Public Library

Mayor William L. Cabell
(1874–1880)(1882–1884)

Mayor Ben Cabell
(1900–1904)

Photos courtesy Dallas Public Library

Mayor Earle Cabell (1961–1964)
in first TV political debate in Dallas

96

Mayor R.L. Thornton (1953–1961)
Courtesy Dallas Public Library

Mayor J. Erik Jonsson (1964–1971)
Courtesy Gittings

World Trade Center
Courtesy Dallas Convention and Visitors Bureau

Dallas-Ft. Worth International Airport
Courtesy Dallas Convention and Visitors Bureau

I.M. Pei-designed City Hall
Courtesy Dallas Convention and Visitors Bureau

J. Erik Jonsson Library
Courtesy Dallas Convention and Visitors Bureau

Cotton Bowl – "The House that Doak built"
Courtesy Dallas Convention and Visitors Bureau

Reunion Arena
Courtesy Dallas Convention and Visitors Bureau

Dallas Skyline
Courtesy Dallas Convention and Visitors Bureau

Morton H. Meyerson Symphony Center
Courtesy Richard DeWeese

101

Mayor Wes Wise (1971–1976)
Courtesy Gittings

Mayor Robert S. Folsom (1976–1981)
Courtesy Gittings

Mayor Jack Evans (1981–1983)
Courtesy Gittings

Mayor Starke Taylor (1983–1987)
Courtesy Gittings

Mayor Annette Strauss (1987–1991)
Courtesy Gittings

Official Seal of the City of Dallas
Courtesy City of Dallas

Texas Stadium
Courtesy Dallas Convention and Visitors Bureau

Dallas Convention Center (foreground)
Courtesy City of Dallas

Big Tex
State Fair of Texas
Courtesy Dallas Convention and Visitors Bureau

EARLY DALLAS MAYORS
MAYOR-ALDERMAN SYSTEM

Approximate Dates:

1856   Dr. Samuel B. Pryor

1857   John M. Crockett

1868   Ben Long

1870   Henry S. Ervay

1872   Ben Long

1874   W.L. Cabell

1880   Dr. J.W. Crowdus

1882   W.L. Cabell

1884   John Henry Brown

1888   Winship "Bud" Connor

1894   Bryan T. Barry

1896   Frank P. Holland

1898   John H. Traylor

1900   Ben E. Cabbell

1904   Bryan T. Barry

1906   Curtis T. Smith

1908   S.J. Hay

MAYOR-COMMISSIONER

1911–1913

Election: April 4, 1911
Votes Cast: 11,358

Mayor: W.M. Holland

Commissioners:

No. 1   J.E. Lee (Streets and Public Property)
No. 2   F.W. Bartlett (Police and Fire) resigned 1-1-13
        L. Blaylock (appointed 1-1-13)
No. 3   W.T. Henderson (Finance and Revenue)
No. 4   R.R. Nelms – Mayor Pro Tem (Waterworks and Sewerage)

City Secretary: J.B. Winslett

❖

1913–1915

Election: April 1, 1913
Votes Cast: 4,960

Mayor: W.M. Holland

Commissioners:

No. 1   L. Blaylock (Police and Fire)
No. 2   S.B. Scott (Streets and Public Property)
No. 3   W.T. Henderson (Finance and Revenue)
No. 4   R.R. Nelms – Mayor Pro Tem (Waterworks and Sewerage)

City Secretary: J.B. Winslett

MAYOR-COMMISSIONER

1915–1917

Election: April 6, 1915
Votes Cast: 12,594

Mayor: Henry D. Lindsley

Commissioners:

No. 1 Manning B. Shannon (Finance and Revenue)
No. 2 Otto H. Lang – Mayor Pro Tem (Streets and Public Property)
No. 3 A.C. Cason (Waterworks and Sewerage)
No. 4 Richard L. Winfrey (Police and Fire)

City Secretary: J.B. Winslett (died Jan. 1917)
                W.W. Peevey (appointed 1-17-17)

❖

1917–1919

Election: April 3, 1917
Votes Cast: 14,371

Mayor: Joe E. Lawther

Commissioners:

No. 1 Otto H. Lang (Streets and Public Property) resigned 4-8-19
No. 2 Wm. Doran (Finance and Revenue)
No. 3 A.C. Cason (Waterworks and Sewerage) resigned 2-3-19
No. 4 Richard L. Winfrey – Mayor Pro Tem (Police and Fire)
             resigned 4-1-18
       T.J. Britton (appointed 4-19-18)

City Secretary: W.W. Peevey

MAYOR-COMMISSIONER

1919–1921

Election: April 1, 1919

Mayor: Frank W. Wozencraft

Commissioners:

No. 1 E.B. Rappert (Finance and Revenue) resigned 6-30-20
No. 2 Hal Moseley (Streets and Public Property)
No. 3 Fred Appel – Mayor Pro Tem (Waterworks and Sewerage)
No. 4 L.E. McGee (Police and Fire)

City Secretary: W.W. Peevey (resigned 9-30-19)
M.G. James (appointed 9-30-19)

❖

1921–1923

Election: April 5, 1921

Mayor: Sawnie R. Aldredge

Commissioners:

No. 1 L. Blaylock – Mayor Pro Tem (Finance and Revenue)
No. 2 J.D. Rose (Streets and Public Property)
No. 3 Fred Appel (Waterworks and Sewerage)
No. 4 L.S. Turley (Police and Fire)

City Secretary: M.G. James

MAYOR-COMMISSIONER

1923–1925

Election: April 3, 1923

Mayor: L. Blaylock

Commissioners:

No. 1   John C. Harris – Mayor Pro Tem (Finance and Revenue)
No. 2   R.A. Wylie (Streets and Public Property)
No. 3   Harry H. Gowens (Waterworks and Sewerage)
No. 4   L.S. Turley (Police and Fire)

City Secretary: M.G. James

❖

1925–1927

Election: April 7, 1925

Mayor: L. Blaylock

Commissioners:

No. 1   John C. Harris – Mayor Pro Tem (Finance and Revenue)
No. 2   R.A. Wylie (Streets and Public Property)
No. 3   Harry H. Gowens (Waterworks and Sewerage)
No. 4   L.S. Turley (Police and Fire)

City Secretary: M.G. James

MAYOR-COMMISSIONER

1927–1929

Election: April 5, 1927

Mayor: R.E. Burt

Commissioners:

No. 1   J. Barney Davis (Finance and Revenue)
No. 2   A.J. Reinhart (Streets and Public Property)
No. 3   S.E. Moss (Waterworks and Sewerage)
No. 4   Clarence S. Parker – Mayor Pro Tem (Police and Fire)

City Secretary: M.G. James
Earl Goforth (appointed 9-15-28)

❖

1929–1931

Election: April 2, 1929

Mayor: J. Waddy Tate

Commissioners:

No. 1   John C. Harris – Mayor Pro Tem (Finance and Revenue)
No. 2   R.A. Wylie (Streets and Public Property)
No. 3   John M. Fouts (Waterworks and Sewerage) resigned 9-1-30
No. 4   W.C. Graves (Police and Fire)

City Secretary: Earl Goforth

COUNCIL-MANAGER

1931–1933

Election: April 7, 1931
Votes Cast: 10,243
Mayor: T.L. Bradford (died August 1932)
       Charles E. Turner (August 31, 1932)
Councilmen:

Place No. 1	A.B. Moore
Place No. 2	H.C. Burroughs
Place No. 3	Victor E. Hexter – Mayor Pro Tem
Place No. 4	W.H. Painter
Place No. 5	E.R. Brown (resigned 11-6-31)
	M.J. Norrell (appointed 12-9-31)
Place No. 6	T.M. Cullum
Place No. 7	Charles E. Turner – Mayor Pro Tem
Place No. 8	Joe C. Thompson
Place No. 9	T.L. Bradford (died August 1932)
	Alex Camp (appointed 9-21-32)
City Manager:	John N. Edy
City Secretary:	Earl Goforth
City Attorney:	James J. Collins

❖

1933–1935

Election: April 4, 1933
Votes Cast: 18,721
Mayor: Charles E. Turner
Councilmen:

Place No. 1	A.B. Moore
Place No. 2	H.C. Burroughs
Place No. 3	Victor H. Hexter – Mayor Pro Tem
Place No. 4	W.H. Painter
Place No. 5	M.J. Norrell
Place No. 6	Wm. Alfred Webb
Place No. 7	Charles E. Turner
Place No. 8	Joe C. Thompson
Place No. 9	Alex Camp
City Manager:	John Edy
City Secretary:	Earl Goforth
City Attorney:	Hugh S. Grady

113

COUNCIL-MANAGER

1935–1937

Election: April 2, 1935
Votes Cast: 20,802

Mayor: George Sergeant
Councilmen:
Place No. 1   George A. Sprague
Place No. 2   J. Willis Gunn
Place No. 3   Emil Corenbleth
Place No. 4   D.R. Graham – Mayor Pro Tem
Place No. 5   J. Cleve Reach
Place No. 6   James F. Cochran
Place No. 7   P.M. Brinker
Place No. 8   Max Hahn
Place No. 9   George Sergeant
City Manager: Hal Mosely
City Secretary: Earl Goforth
City Attorney: H.P. Kucera

❖

1937-1939

Election: April 6, 1937
Votes Cast: 14,227

Mayor: George A. Sprague
Councilmen:
Place No. 1   George A. Sprague
Place No. 2   J. Willis Gunn
Place No. 3   Emil Corenbleth
Place No. 4   D. R. Graham – Mayor Pro Tem
Place No. 5   Z. Starr Armstrong
Place No. 6   Hughes Knight
Place No. 7   P. M. Brinker
Place No. 8   Max Hahn (died July 28, 1938)
              J. Cleve Reach (appointed August 1, 1938)
Place No. 9   George Sergeant
City Manager: Hal Moseley
City Secretary: Earl Goforth
City Attorney: H.P. Kucera

114

COUNCIL-MANAGER

1939 -1941
Election: April 4, 1939
Votes Cast: 20,368
Mayor: Woodall Rodgers
Councilmen:

Place No. 1	W.B. Johnson
Place No. 2	M.M. Straus
Place No. 3	L.L. Hiegel
Place No. 4	Bennett H. Stampes
Place No. 5	Ben E. Cabell, Jr. – Mayor Pro Tem
Place No. 6	W. Hal Noble
Place No. 7	Woodall Rodgers
Place No. 8	C.P. Haynes (died November 1939)
	E.J. Gannon (appointed 11-8-39)
Place No. 9	R.D. Suddarth
City Manager:	Hal Moseley (released 7-1-39)
	James W. Aston (appointed 8-1-39)
City Secretary:	Earl Goforth
City Attorney:	H.P. Kucera

❖

1941–1943
Election: April 1, 1941
Votes Cast: 10,544
Mayor: Woodall Rodgers
Councilmen:

Place No. 1	W. B. Johnson
Place No. 2	M. M. Straus
Place No. 3	L. L. Hiegel
Place No. 4	Bennett H. Stampes
Place No. 5	Ben E. Cabell, Jr. (Mayor Pro Tem) resigned 3-10-43
	O.D. Brundridge (appointed 3-10-43)
Place No. 6	Hal Noble (resigned 2-17-43)
	W.C. McCord (appointed 2-24-43)
Place No. 7	Woodall Rodgers
Place No. 8	E.J. Gannon, Jr. (died Feb. 1943)
	J.B. Adoue (appointed 3-4-42) Mayor Pro Tem
Place No. 9	O.W. Cox
City Manager:	James W. Aston (on military leave)
	V.R. Smitham (acting city manager)
City Secretary:	Earl Goforth
City Attorney:	H.P. Kucera

COUNCIL-MANAGER

1943–1945

Election: April 6, 1943
Votes Cast: 2,899 (no opposition)

Mayor: Woodall Rodgers
Councilmen:
Place No. 1   W.B. Johnson
Place No. 2   M.M. Straus
Place No. 3   L.L. Hiegel
Place No. 4   Bennett H. Stampes
Place No. 5   Oscar D. Brundridge
Place No. 6   W.C. McCord
Place No. 7   Woodall Rodgers
Place No. 8   J.B. Adoue, Jr. – Mayor Pro Tem
Place No. 9   O.W. Cox
City Manager: James W. Aston (on military leave)
                V.R. Smitham (acting city manager)
City Secretary: Earl Goforth
City Attorney: H.P. Kucera

❖

1945–1947

Election: April 3, 1945
Votes Cast: 4,749 (no opposition)

Mayor: Woodall Rodgers
Councilmen:
Place No. 1   W.B. Johnson
Place No. 2   M.M. Straus
Place No. 3   L.L. Hiegel
Place No. 4   Bennett H. Stampes
Place No. 5   O.D. Brundridge
Place No. 6   W.C. McCord
Place No. 7   Woodall Rodgers
Place No. 8   J.B. Adoue, Jr. – Mayor Pro Tem
Place No. 9   O.W. Cox
City Manager: James W. Aston (on military leave)(resigned 12-5-45)
                V.R. Smitham (acting)(appointed 12-5-45)
City Secretary: Earl Goforth
City Attorney: H.P. Kucera

COUNCIL-MANAGER

1947–1949
Election: April 1, 1947
Votes Cast: 21,977
Mayor: J.R. Temple
Councilmen:

Place No. 1	W.J. Red Bryan (resigned 2-17-48)
	Jess S. Epps (appointed 2-24-48)
Place No. 2	Roland L. Pelt
Place No. 3	C.G. Stubbs, Sr.
Place No. 4	Robert H. Lindop
Place No. 5	Wallace H. Savage – Mayor Pro Tem
Place No. 6	Everett C. Fox
Place No. 7	E.C. Harrell
Place No. 8	Ashley DeWitt (resigned 12-9-47)
	William S. Brown (appointed 12-9-47)
Place No. 9	J.R. Temple
City Manager:	Roderic B. Thomas
City Secretary:	Earl Goforth
City Attorney:	H.P. Kucera

❖

1949–1951
Election: April 5, 1949
Votes Cast: 23,629
Mayor: Wallace H. Savage
Councilmen:

Place No. 1	Jess S. Epps
Place No. 2	Roland L. Pelt (resigned 4-18-50)
	Percy L. Carpenter (appointed 4-18-50)
Place No. 3	C.G. Stubbs, Sr.–Mayor Pro-Tem
Place No. 4	Robert H. Lindop
Place No. 5	Wallace H. Savage
Place No. 6	Dr. Harold A. O'Brien
Place No. 7	E.C. Harrell
Place No. 8	J.B. Adoue, Jr.
Place No. 9	W.H. Pierce
City Manager:	Roderic B. Thomas
	Charles A. Ford (appointed 1-1-50)
City Secretary:	Earl Goforth
	Harold G. Shank (appointed 11-15-50)
City Attorney:	H.P. Kucera

COUNCIL-MANAGER

1951–1953
Election: April 3, 1951
Votes Cast: 14,379
Mayor: J.B. Adoue, Jr.
Councilmen:
Place No. 1   Jess S. Epps – Mayor Pro Tem (11-26-52)
Place No. 2   Percy L. Carpenter – Mayor Pro Tem (12-11-51)
           (resigned 11-26-52)
           Harold B. Wright (appted 11-26-52)
           (resigned 1-31-53)
           T.M. Schrock (appointed 2-3-53)
Place No. 3   Bernard B. Hemphill, Jr.
Place No. 4   L.H. Ridout, Jr. (resigned 11-14-52)
           Clarence B. Kloppe (appointed 11-14-52)
Place No. 5   George A. Schenewerk
Place No. 6   Cecil D. French
Place No. 7   A. Azel Adams
Place No. 8   W.H. Pierce – Mayor Pro Tem (resigned 12-4-51)
           W.B. Ring (appointed 12-4-51)
Place No. 9   J.B. Adoue, Jr.
City Manager: Charles C. Ford (resigned 5-15-52)
           Elgin E. Crull (appointed 5-15-52)
City Secretary: Harold G. Shank
City Attorney: H.P. Kucera

❖

1953–1955
Election: April 7, 1953
Votes Cast: 31,586
Mayor: R.L. Thornton, Sr.
Councilmen:
Place No. 1   O.H. Vickrey
Place No. 2   J.R. "Cap" Terry
Place No. 3   Milton Richardson
Place No. 4   Roderic B. Thomas
Place No. 5   W.C. "Dub" Miller
Place No. 6   Arthur L. Kramer, Jr.
Place No. 7   William J. "Bill" Harris
Place No. 8   Vernon S. Smith – Mayor Pro Tem
Place No. 9   R.L. Thornton, Sr.
City Manager: Elgin E. Crull
City Secretary: Harold G. Shank
City Attorney: H.P. Kucera

COUNCIL-MANAGER

1955–1957

Election: April 5, 1955
Votes Cast: 2,213 (no opposition)

Mayor: R.L. Thornton, Sr.
Councilmen:
Place No. 1   O.H. Vickrey
Place No. 2   J.R. "Cap" Terry
Place No. 3   Milton Richardson
Place No. 4   Roderic B. Thomas (resigned 5-16-55)
      Tom L. Beauchamp, Jr. (appointed 5-16-55)
Place No. 5   W.C. "Dub" Miller
Place No. 6   Arthur L. Kramer, Jr.
Place No. 7   William J. "Bill" Harris
Place No. 8   Vernon S. Smith – Mayor Pro Tem
Place No. 9   R.L. Thornton, Sr.
City Manager: Elgin E. Crull
City Secretary: Harold G. Shank
City Attorney: H.P. Kucera

❖

1957–1959

Election: April 2, 1957
Votes Cast: 61,986

Mayor: R.L. Thornton, Sr.
Council Members:
Place No. 1   O.H. Vickrey
Place No. 2   J.R. "Cap" Terry
Place No. 3   Milton Richardson
Place No. 4   Tom L. Beauchamp, Jr.
Place No. 5   W.C. "Dub" Miller
Place No. 6   Mrs. Carr P. Collins, Jr.
Place No. 7   Tom Unis
Place No. 8   Vernon S. Smith – Mayor Pro Tem
Place No. 9   R.L. Thornton, Sr.
City Manager: Elgin E. Crull
City Secretary: Harold G. Shank
City Attorney: H.P. Kucera

COUNCIL-MANAGER

1959–1961

Election: April 7, 1959
Votes Cast: 60,036

Mayor: R.L. Thornton, Sr.
Council Members:
Place No. 1   Teddy Harris
Place No. 2   Dr. R.A. Self
Place No. 3   N.E. McKinney
Place No. 4   Joe Geary
Place No. 5   Walter H. Cousins, Jr.
Place No. 6   Mrs. Carr P. Collins, Jr.
Place No. 7   George F. Mixon, Sr.
Place No. 8   Elgin B. Robertson, Sr. – Mayor Pro Tem
Place No. 9   R. L. Thornton, Sr.
City Manager: Elgin E. Crull
City Secretary: Harold G. Shank
City Attorney: H.P. Kucera

❖

1961–1963

Election: April 4, 1961
Votes Cast: 82,209

Mayor: Earle Cabell
Council Members:
Place No. 1   Carrie E. Welch
Place No. 2   Dr. R.A. Self
Place No. 3   Joe G. Moody
Place No. 4   Mrs. Elizabeth Blessing
Place No. 5   Walter H. Cousins, Jr. (resigned 11-19-62)
                  Joe H. Golman (appointed 11-19-62)
Place No. 6   George M. Underwood, Jr.
Place No. 7   Charles S. Sharp
Place No. 8   Elgin B. Robertson, Sr. – Mayor Pro Tem
Place No. 9   Earle Cabell
City Manager: Elgin E. Crull
City Secretary: Harold G. Shank
City Attorney: H.P. Kucera

COUNCIL-MANAGER

1963–1965
Election: April 2, 1963
Votes Cast: 61,769
Mayor: Earle Cabell (resigned 2-3-64)
      J. Erik Jonsson (appointed 2-3-64)
Council Members:

Place No. 1	Carrie P. Welch – Mayor Pro Tem
Place No. 2	W.H. (Bill) Roberts
Place No. 3	Joe G. Moody
Place No. 4	Mrs. Elizabeth Blessing
Place No. 5	Joe H. Golman
Place No. 6	George M. Underwood, Jr.
Place No. 7	Mrs. Tracy H. Rutherford
Place No. 8	R.B. Carpenter, Jr.
Place No. 9	Earle Cabell (resigned 2-3-64)
	J. Erik Jonsson (appointed 2-3-64)
City Manager:	Elgin B. Crull
City Secretary:	Harold G. Shank
City Attorney:	H.P. Kucera

❖

1965–1967
Election: April 6, 1965
Votes cast: 80,791
Mayor: J. Erik Jonsson
Council Members:

Place No. 1	Frank A. Hoke
Place No. 2	W.H. (Bill) Roberts
Place No. 3	Joe G. Moody (resigned 2-12-67)
	C. A. Galloway (appointed 3-20-67)
Place No. 4	William E. Cothrum
Place No. 5	Joe H. Golman – Deputy Mayor Pro Tem
Place No. 6	Charles G. Cullum
Place No. 7	Mrs. C.F. (Sibyl) Hamilton
Place No. 8	R.B. Carpenter, Jr. – Mayor Pro Tem
Place No. 9	J. Erik Jonsson
City Manager:	Elgin E. Crull (resigned 6-30-66)
	W.S. McDonald (appointed 7-14-66)
City Secretary:	Harold G. Shank
City Attorney:	H.P. Kucera (resigned 6-21-65)
	N. Alex Bickley (appointed 6-28-65)

COUNCIL-MANAGER

1967–1969
Election: April 4, 1967
Votes Cast: 23,438
Mayor: J. Erik Jonsson
Council Members:
Place No. 1 (1)*   Frank A. Hoke – Mayor Pro Tem
Place No. 2 (2)*   Abe Meyer
Place No. 3 (7)*   Jesse Price
Place No. 4 (6)*   William E. Cothrum
Place No. 5 (4)*   Jack Moser
Place No. 6 (3)*   Charles G. Cullum – Deputy Mayor Pro Tem
Place No. 7 (9)*   Mrs. C.F. (Sibyl) Hamilton
Place No. 8 (10)*   Jack F. McKinney
Place No. 9 (11)*   J. Erik Jonsson
Place No. (5)*   Henry Stuart **(appointed 12-2-68)
Place No. (8)*   George L. Allen**(appointed 12-2-68)
*Council place numbers in accordance with City Charter adopted 10-22-68
**Additional Council Places created by City Charter adopted 10-22-68
City Manager: W.S. McDonald
City Secretary: Harold G. Shank
City Attorney: N. Alex Bickley

❖

1969–1971
Election: April 1, 1969
Votes Cast: 42,613
Mayor: J. Erik Jonsson
Council Members:
Place No. 1   Ted Holland
Place No. 2   Abe Meyer
Place No. 3   Doug Fain
Place No. 4   Gary Weber
Place No. 5   Wes Wise
Place No. 6   Sheffield Kadane – Deputy Mayor Pro Tem
Place No. 7   Jesse Price
Place No. 8   George Allen
Place No. 9   Mrs. Alfred (Anita) Martinez
Place No. 10   Jack F. McKinney – Mayor Pro Tem
Place No. 11   J. Erik Jonsson
City Manager: W.S. McDonald
City Secretary: Harold G. Shank
City Attorney: N. Alex Bickley

COUNCIL-MANAGER

1971–1973
Election: April 6, 1971
Votes Cast: 76,616
Mayor: Wes Wise
Council Members:

Place No. 1	Ted Holland – Mayor Pro Tem
Place No. 2	Jerry Gilmore
Place No. 3	Doug Fain – Deputy Mayor Pro Tem
Place No. 4	Garry Weber
Place No. 5	Russell B. Smith
Place No. 6	Sheffield Kadane
Place No. 7	Jesse Price (resigned 1-31-72)
	Lawrence Ackels (appointed 2-7-72)
Place No. 8	George Allen
Place No. 9	Mrs. Alfred (Anita) Martinez
Place No. 10	Fred Zeder
Place No. 11	Wes Wise
City Manager:	W.S. McDonald (resigned 11-6-72)
	George Schrader (appointed 12-18-72)
City Secretary:	Harold G. Shank
City Attorney:	N. Alex Bickley

❖

1973–1975
Election: April 3, 1973
Votes Cast: 51,688
Mayor: Wes Wise
Council Members:

Place No. 1	Charles H. Storey
Place No. 2	Jerry Gilmore
Place No. 3	Mrs. Adlene Harrison
Place No. 4	Garry Weber
Place No. 5	Russell B. Smith – Deputy Mayor Pro Tem
Place No. 6	George Allen – Mayor Pro Tem
Place No. 7	L.A. Murr
Place No. 8	Mrs. Lucy Patterson
Place No. 9	Pedro Aguirre
Place No. 10	Charles Terrell
Place No. 11	Wes Wise
City Manager:	George Schrader
City Secretary:	Harold G. Shank
City Attorney:	N. Alex Bickley

COUNCIL-MANAGER

1975–1977
Election: April 1, 1975   Votes Cast: 81,670
Mayor: Wes Wise (resigned 1-30-76)
      Robert S. Folsom (elected 4-26-76)
Council Members:

Place No. 1	Mrs. Rose Renfroe
Place No. 2	William F. (Bill) Nicol
Place No. 3	John N. Leedom
Place No. 4	Richard Smith
Place No. 5	William Cothrum
Place No. 6	George Allen – Mayor Pro Tem (resigned 9-22-75)
	Mrs. Juanita Craft (elected 12-24-75)
Place No. 7	L.A. Murr – Deputy Mayor Pro Tem (1-12-76)
Place No. 8	Mrs. Lucy Patterson
Place No. 9	Garry Weber (resigned 2-2-76)
	Bill Blackburn (elected 4-26-76)
Place No. 10	Mrs. Adlene Harrison – Deputy Mayor Pro Tem; Mayor Pro Tem 1-12-76
Place No. 11	Wes Wise (resigned 1-30-76)
	Bob Folsom (elected 4-26-76)
City Manager:	George Schrader
City Secretary:	Harold G. Shank (retired 12-29-76)
	Robert S. Sloan (appointed 11-22-76)
City Attorney:	N. Alex Bickley (resigned 7-31-76)
	Lee E. Holt (appointed 8-2-76)

❖

1977–1979
Election: April 2, 1977
Mayor: Robert S. Folsom
Council Members:

Place No. 1	Don Hicks
Place No. 2	William F. (Bill) Nicol
Place No. 3	John N. Leedom
Place No. 4	Richard (Dick) Smith
Place No. 5	William Cothrum
Place No. 6	Juanita Craft
Place No. 7	Dr. John A. Walton (resigned 5-23-79)
Place No. 8	Lucy Patterson
Place No. 9	Bill Blackburn
Place No. 10	Adlene Harrison (resigned 8-31-77)
	Steve Bartlett (elected 11-8-77)
Place No. 11	Robert S. Folsom
City Manager:	George Schrader
City Secretary:	Robert S. Sloan
City Attorney:	Lee E. Holt

COUNCIL-MANAGER

1980–1981

Election: Jan. 19, 1980

Mayor: Robert S. Folsom
Council Members:
Place No. 1   Don Hicks
Place No. 2   Ricardo Medrano
Place No. 3   Joe Haggar
Place No. 4   Rolan Tucker
Place No. 5   Lee Simpson
Place No. 6   Elsie Faye Heggins
Place No. 7   Max Goldblatt
Place No. 8   Fred Blair
Place No. 9   Sid Stahl
Place No. 10   Steve Bartlett
Place No. 11   Robert S. Folsom
City Manager: George Schrader
City Secretary: Robert S. Sloan
City Attorney: Lee E. Holt

❖

1981–1982

Election: April 4, 1981
Mayor: Jack Evans
Council Members:
Place No. 1   Don Hicks
Place No. 2   Ricardo Medrano
Place No. 3   Joe Haggar
Place No. 4   Roland Tucker
Place No. 5   Lee Simpson
Place No. 6   Elsie Faye Heggins
Place No. 7   Max Goldblatt
Place No. 8   Fred Blair
Place No. 9   Sid Stahl
Place No. 10   Wes Wise
Place No. 11   Jack Evans
City Manager: Charles Anderson (appointed 10-1-81)
City Secretary: Robert S. Sloan
City Attorney: Lee E. Holt
                 Analeslie Muncy (appointed 8-17-82)

COUNCIL-MANAGER

1983–1985
Election: April 2, 1983
Votes Cast: 85,861
Mayor: Starke Taylor
Council Members:

Place No. 1	Jim Hart
Place No. 2	Paul Fielding
Place No. 3	Jim Richards
Place No. 4	Dean Vanderbilt
Place No. 5	Craig Holcomb
Place No. 6	Elsie Faye Heggins
Place No. 7	Max Goldblatt
Place No. 8	Fred Blair
Place No. 9	Jerry Rucker
Place No. 10	Annette Strauss
Place No. 11	Starke Taylor
City Manager:	Charles S. Anderson
City Secretary:	Robert Sloan
City Attorney:	Analeslie Muncy

❖

1985–1987
Election: April 6, 1986
Mayor: Starke Taylor
Council Members:

Place No. 1	Bill Milkie
Place No. 2	Lori Palmer
Place No. 3	Jim Richards
Place No. 4	Dean Vanderbilt
Place No. 5	Craig Holcomb
Place No. 6	Diane Ragsdale – Deputy Mayor Pro Tem
Place No. 7	John Evans
Place No. 8	Al Lipscomb
Place No. 9	Jerry Rucker
Place No. 10	Annette Strauss – Mayor Pro Tem
Place No. 11	Starke Taylor
City Manager:	Charles Anderson (resigned)
	Richard S. Knight (appointed 11-1-86)
City Secretary:	Robert Sloan
City Attorney:	Analeslie Muncy

COUNCIL-MANAGER

1987–1989
Election: April 4, 1987
Votes Cast: 114,186
Mayor: Annette Strauss
Council Members:

Place No. 1	Charles Tandy
Place No. 2	Lori Palmer
Place No. 3	Jerry Bartos
Place No. 4	Dean Vanderbilt
	Max Wells (7-18-89)
Place No. 5	Craig Holcomb
Place No. 6	Diane Ragsdale – Deputy Mayor Pro Tem
Place No. 7	John Evans – Mayor Pro Tem
Place No. 8	Al Lipscomb
Place No. 9	Jerry Rucker
Place No. 10	Al Gonzalez
Place No. 11	Annette Strauss
City Manager:	Richard S. Knight
City Secretary:	Robert Sloan
City Attorney:	Analeslie Muncy

❖

1989 - 1991
Election: May 6, 1989   Votes Cast: 89,064
Mayor: Annette Strauss
Council Members:

Place No. 1	Charles Tandy
Place No. 2	Lori Palmer
Place No. 3	Jerry Bartos
Place No. 4	Max W. Wells
Place No. 5	Glenn Box
Place No. 6	Diane Ragsdale – Deputy Mayor Pro Tem
Place No. 7	John Evans – Mayor Pro Tem
Place No. 8	Al Lipscomb
Place No. 9	Harriet Miers
Place No. 10	Jim Buerger
Place No. 11	Annette Strauss
City Manager:	Richard Knight (resigned 4-27-90)
	Jan Hart (appointed 4-27-90)
City Secretary:	Robert Sloan
City Attorney:	Analeslie Muncy

REFERENCES

Acheson, Sam, *Dallas Yesterday*, S.M.U. Press, Dallas 1977.

Barta, Carolyn, *The Dallas News and Council-Manager Government*, The University of Texas, Austin, 1970.

Boykin, Lucy, and Brinkerhoff, Mary, *Text to Tower*, Dallas Public Library, 1982.

Dealey, Ted, Diaper *Days of Dallas*, Abdingdon Press, Nashville, New York, 1966.

Greene, A.C. , *A Place Called Dallas*, Dallas County Heritage Society, Inc., Dallas, 1975.

Kimball, Justin, *Our City Dallas*, Dallas Independent School, District, Dallas, 1975.

Leslie, Warren, *Dallas Public and Private*, Crossman Publishers, New York, 1964.

Lewis, Arthur, *Fortune Magazine*, November 1968.

Lyons, Douglas C., *The Dallas Times Herald*, November 21, 1986.

Mayors Oral History Project, East Texas State University,
Dallas Public Library:

Aston, James	Folsom, Robert
Bickley, Alex	Greene, A.C.
Blessing, Elizabeth	Kucera, H.P.
Cullum, Charles	Savage, Wallace
Cullum, Robert	Schrader, George
Evans, Jack	Stemmons, John

Oppenheimer, Evelyn, Potterfield, Bill, editors, *The Book of Dallas*, Doubleday and Company, Inc., New York, 1976.

Payne, Darwin, *Dallas: An Illustrated History*, Windsor Publications Inc., Woodland Hills, CA, 1982.

Saxon, Gerald D. *Reminiscences: A Glimpse of Old East Dallas*, Dallas Public Library, 1983.

Sharpe, Ernest, *G.B. Dealey of the Dallas News*, Henry Holt and Company, New York, 1955.

Tinkle, Lon, *The Key to Dallas*, J.B. Lippincott Company, Philadelphia and New York, 1965.

Trent, Lucy, *John Neely Bryan: Founder of Dallas*, Tardy Publishing Co., Dallas, TX, 1936.

Welch, June, *Riding Fence*, GLA Press, Dallas, Texian Press, Waco, 1983

Wise, Mayor Wes, Personal Interviews, November 2, 8, 16, 1984.

ABOUT THE AUTHOR

Allison A. Cheney

Allison A. Cheney, a fourth generation Dallas native, developed her love and pride for Dallas at a very young age. Her interests and activities in city politics followed shortly.

Cheney established her versatility early as a student at Ursuline Academy, the University of Oklahoma, and the University of Dallas. She was active in journalism, public speaking, debate, and political science. She won numerous awards in journalism and government at all three institutions, including The Future Journalists of America award for best political editorial at the University of Oklahoma.

While a high school student in 1976, Cheney represented the city of Dallas as a special guest to the National Bicentennial activities and ceremonies in Philadelphia and New York City.

After receiving her Bachelor of Arts degree in history at the University of Dallas, Cheney moved to Washington, D.C. to work in the office of Senator Edward M. Kennedy. While in Washington, she was active in the Texas State Society, the Senatorial Leadership Circle, and was a guest of First Lady Nancy Reagan at the White House.

Returning to Dallas, Cheney became vice-president of her family's business, and resumed her involvement in Dallas politics. She served on Dallas County District Attorney Henry Wade's final grand jury, and Mayor Annette Strauss appointed her to the Motion Picture Classification Board of the city of Dallas.

Cheney currently is heard on radio stations KAAM/ KZPS. She is a regular on the popular "Breakfast Club" on KAAM, and her analysis of movies, "Allison Cheney at the Movies" is a special attraction every Friday morning. She also interviews entertainment personalities and political figures. At the present time, both stations are featuring her vignettes about Dallas history for the Jubilee Dallas celebration.

Cheney's first book, *A Legacy of Love,* is a genealogy of her family, and won the First Place Award from the Dallas Genealogy Society. *Dallas Spirit* is Cheney's second book.

❖